OMBAT AIRCRAFT

138 RAF TORNADO UNITS OF GULF WAR I

SERIES EDITOR TONY HOLMES

138

COMBAT
AIRCRAFT

Michael Napier

RAF TORNADO UNITS OF GULF WAR I

OSPREY
PUBLISHING

OSPREY PUBLISHING
Bloomsbury Publishing Plc
Kemp House, Chawley Park, Cumnor Hill, Oxford OX2 9PH, UK
29 Earlsfort Terrace, Dublin 2, Ireland
1385 Broadway, 5th Floor, New York, NY 10018, USA
Email: info@ospreypublishing.com
www.ospreypublishing.com

Osprey Publishing is a division of Bloomsbury Publishing Plc

First published in Great Britain in 2021

A catalogue record for this book is available from the British Library.

ISBN: PB 9781472845115; eBook 9781472845108;
ePDF 9781472845122; XML 9781472845092

21 22 23 24 25   10 9 8 7 6 5 4 3 2

Edited by Tony Holmes
Cover artwork by Gareth Hector
Aircraft profiles by Janusz Światłoń
Index by Alan Rutter
Originated by PDQ Digital Media Solutions, UK
Printed and bound in India by Replika Press Private Ltd.

Osprey Publishing supports the Woodland Trust, the UK's leading woodland
conservation charity.

To find out more about our authors and books visit **www.ospreypublishing.com**.
Here you will find extracts, author interviews, details of forthcoming events and
the option to sign up for our newsletter.

Acknowledgements
My thanks to the following for their contributions – Pete Batson, David Bellamy,
Euan Black, Ian Black, Gordon Buckley, Steve Cockram, Chris Coulls, Mal Craghill,
Jim Crowley, Angus Elliott, Andy Glover, Wally Grout, Simon Hadley, David
Hamilton, Rod Hawkins, Nick Heard, Les Hendry, Rich Jones, Paul Lightbody,
Mike Lumb, Tim Marsh, Bob McAlpine, Paul McKernan, Andy Moir, Kev Noble,
Stu Osborne, Mark Paisey, Rick Peacock-Edwards, Nigel Risdale, Lars Smith, Chris
Stradling, Roy Trotter, Jerry Ward, Martin Wintermeyer and the late Jerry Witts.

Front Cover
On the evening of 17 January 1991, the
Tabuk Wing was tasked with mounting
Mission 2621/G against the runway
surfaces at Al Asad air base in central Iraq.
Sqn Ldr P K Batson and Wg Cdr M C Heath
led the eight Tornado GR 1s of Dundee
formation – all of which were armed with
JP233 runway denial weapons – that
targeted the airfield. This original artwork by
artist Gareth Hector captures the scene
when Batson and Heath, in Tornado GR 1
ZA447/EA, streaked over the airfield at
500 knots delivering their weapons across
the runway. Visible in the background is an
Iraqi Air Force Mirage F1EQ that was
destroyed after landing on the runway
moments before the attack (*Cover artwork
by Gareth Hector*)

Previous Spread
A trio of Tornado GR 1s armed with Hunting
JP233 runway denial weapons. Most crews
had the opportunity to fly the aircraft in this
heavy and draggy configuration before
combat operations commenced
(*Mike Lumb*)

CONTENTS

CHAPTER ONE

PREPARATION FOR WAR

When the Cold War ended in December 1989, the Royal Air Force (RAF) was completing a major re-equipment programme that had been started eight years previously. A single aircraft type had been introduced to replace the Avro Vulcan, Blackburn Buccaneer, Sepecat Jaguar, English Electric Lightning and McDonnell Douglas Phantom II. By mid-1990, the Panavia Tornado had replaced all five types in the strike/attack, tactical reconnaissance and air defence roles, and equipped 18 frontline squadrons.

Although the Tornado was ostensibly one aircraft type, there were, in fact, two distinct variants, namely the Interdictor Strike (IDS) and Air Defence Variant (ADV). The IDS, known in RAF service as the Tornado GR 1, was designed as a low-level strike/attack aircraft. A Terrain Following Radar (TFR) could be linked to the autopilot system and a Ground Mapping Radar (GMR) could be used to update the navigation/attack system, giving the aircraft a night/all-weather capability. The Tornado GR 1 was powered by two Turbo-Union RB199-101/103 turbofans, which were designed to give an economical fuel burn during low-level cruise.

The high wing-loading of the aircraft's variable-geometry wings ensured a stable weapons platform at low-level. RAF Tornado crews trained exclusively at low-level, practising the delivery of 1000-lb retarded or freefall bombs, or the Hunting JP233 runway denial weapon. The Tornado

Seen on the apron at Leeming, Tornado F 3s from No 11 (Composite) Sqn are readied for deployment to the Gulf on 29 August 1990 (*Tony Paxton*)

GR 1A sub-variant incorporated a tactical reconnaissance system, which, once again, was optimised for low-level flight.

The ADV started life in the RAF as the Tornado F 2 and was delivered to No 229 Operational Conversion Unit (OCU) at Coningsby, in Lincolnshire, in 1985. It was initially equipped with RB199-103 engines and the GEC-Marconi AI.24 Foxhunter radar. Much of the work of an air defence aircraft is carried out at medium-level, and here the performance of the Tornado F 2 suffered because both airframe and engines were optimised for low-level flight. In order to improve the F 2's capabilities at medium- and high-level, the aircraft was fitted with the more powerful RB199-104 engines and, together with the inclusion of a number of other system improvements, was re-designated as the Tornado F 3.

Following a number of essential modifications to the AI.24 Foxhunter radar in order to meet the RAF's operational requirements, and after a lot of hard work meeting all operational work-up requirements, the Tornado F 3 was delivered to NATO as planned, and on time, in December 1986, although the radar still continued to be plagued with problems. The OCU was designated No 65 Sqn, and it became the first operational Tornado F 3 unit, commanded by Wg Cdr R S Peacock-Edwards. In service, the Tornado F 3 was armed with four AIM-9L Sidewinder infra-red heat-seeking Air-to-Air Missiles (AAM) and four BAe Skyflash semi-active radar-guided AAMs. The aircraft was also armed with a 27 mm Mauser cannon with a radar-computed gunsight.

The Tornado GR 1 entered service with No 9 Sqn at Honington, Suffolk, in 1982, followed over the next three years by the strike/attack squadrons at Marham, in Norfolk, and Laarbruch and Brüggen in RAF Germany (RAFG). The final units to receive the Tornado GR 1 were No 2 Sqn at Laarbruch and No 13 Sqn at Honington, which received the GR 1A tactical reconnaissance version in 1988 and 1990, respectively. After its introduction with No 29 Sqn, the Tornado F 3 was progressively deployed by the air defence squadrons at Coningsby, in Lincolnshire, at Leeming, in North Yorkshire, and at Leuchars, in Scotland. By mid-1990, the RAF Air Order of Battle included the following Tornado units;

RAF Germany		
Brüggen	No 9 Sqn	Tornado GR 1
	No 14 Sqn	Tornado GR 1
	No 17 Sqn	Tornado GR 1
	No 31 Sqn	Tornado GR 1
Laarbruch	No 2 Sqn	Tornado GR 1A
	No 15 Sqn	Tornado GR 1
	No 16 Sqn	Tornado GR 1
	No 20 Sqn	Tornado GR 1

RAF Strike Command		
No 1 Group		
Honington	No 13 Sqn	Tornado GR 1A
Marham	No 27 Sqn	Tornado GR 1
	No 617 Sqn	Tornado GR 1

No 11 Group		
Coningsby	No 5 Sqn	Tornado F 3
	No 29 Sqn	Tornado F 3
Leeming	No 11 Sqn	Tornado F 3
	No 23 Sqn	Tornado F 3
	No 25 Sqn	Tornado F 3
Leuchars	No 43 Sqn	Tornado F 3
	No 111 Sqn	Tornado F 3

After the threat from central Europe had evaporated with the ending of the Cold War, the air forces in NATO found themselves without a focus. However, a new adversary soon emerged in the shape of Iraq, which had long-held claims over neighbouring Kuwait. Diplomatic rumblings that had started in 1989 in the Persian Gulf region, when Iraq accused Kuwait of slant drilling into the Rumaylah oil field, exploded into a full international crisis when the Iraqi army invaded Kuwait on 2 August 1990. Determined to liberate Kuwait and to protect the sovereignty of Saudi Arabia, the US sent a task force to the Gulf region and began to assemble an international Coalition. This included British forces, which were also hastily despatched to the Middle East in Operation *Granby*.

On 7 August 1990, No 5 Sqn, under the command of Wg Cdr E J Black, deployed from Coningsby to Akrotiri, on Cyprus, for the unit's annual five-week Armament Practice Camp (APC) to hone its air-to-air gunnery skills in order to qualify to the NATO standard. No 5 Sqn was to replace its sister unit, No 29 Sqn, under the command of Wg Cdr R W D Trotter, which had just completed its APC and was shortly to return to Coningsby. Following the day's final sorties, aircrew from both squadrons celebrated in the usual way with a raucous party in the Akrotiri Officer's Mess.

Wg Cdr Black remembered 'being summoned from the party to the message centre in Ops Wing to be presented with a FLASH message from HQ Strike Command ordering me and OC [Officer Commanding] No 29 Sqn to fully arm 12 aircraft and await further instructions. There were a number of missiles in Cyprus and both squadrons prepared to load their aircraft straight away. There was no indication of where the aircraft would deploy to, but much speculation amongst the aircrew who suspected it might be Bahrain. The 12 best aircraft were selected for deployment, with emphasis on the state of the radars.'

The performance of the AI.24 Foxhunter radar had been upgraded in service by a series of modifications introduced as 'Lists' – the X-List, the Y-List and the Z-List. It was important to select Z-List aircraft with the latest radar modifications. 'In a modern air defence fighter', continued Wg Cdr Black, 'the radar is the brain that controls the eyes, ears and teeth of the weapon system. Without it there is no weapon system. The Z-List radars were the best available at the time, and would later be replaced in-theatre at the first opportunity by aircraft with the next upgrade modifications known as "Stage 1+" radars. For now, however, it was Z-List radars.'

No 29 Sqn pilot Flt Lt E A C Elliott recalled;

'We had a bit of a tense couple of days wondering quite what was in store. No 29 Sqn's ten aircraft in Cyprus were pretty knackered – they

The Tornado F 3s of No 5 Sqn deployed from Cyprus to Dhahran on 11 August. Although the aircraft are not carrying underwing tanks, they are armed with a full load of AAMs. The deployment was accompanied by TriStar and Victor tankers (*Euan Black collection*)

were "Z-List" radar jets, which was an increasingly obsolete standard with a, frankly, pretty useless radar. The jets had spent the previous five weeks doing nothing but gunnery, which was notorious for shaking the weapons system to pieces. There weren't many missiles in Cyprus and the jets were not fitted with any defensive aids.'

The decision to commit the Tornado F 3s to the Gulf was made in London on 8 August. Gp Capt Peacock-Edwards, the station commander at Leeming, was deployed to Saudi Arabia two days later to command the RAF assets in theatre and Sqn Ldr J R Jones of No 5 Sqn left Akrotiri to set up a Tornado F 3 detachment at a yet to be decided base. Three days later, 12 Tornado F 3s and 24 Combat-Ready (CR) crews, drawn from both units, reinforced by five crews from No 11 Sqn at Leeming, arrived at the Royal Saudi Air Force (RSAF) base at Dhahran. The combined unit, known as No 5 (Composite) Sqn, was commanded by Wg Cdr Black.

Early on the morning of 11 August, 12 fully armed F 3s deployed in two waves, each of six aircraft, escorted halfway by a VC10K tanker. The first wave was flown by No 5 Sqn and the second wave by No 29 Sqn. The first leg heading south from Akrotiri to Luxor, in Egypt, was a standard transit in company with the tanker and following the river Nile. At Luxor the tankers returned to Akrotiri and the F 3s turned onto an easterly heading across Saudi Arabia to Dhahran.

'What should have been another standard transit across the desert became slightly more fraught', reported Wg Cdr Black, 'when the F 3s left the tanker radio frequency and were unable to make radio contact with any control agency. Each aircraft in the formation attempted to make contact but to no avail. This persisted for more than an hour with no radio contact, and as we continued heading east, we were coming within range of the Iraq border to the north and the possibility of encountering Iraqi aircraft, so lookout to the north became particularly sharp. Another thought generated by the lack of radio contact was whether the Saudi control agencies might have been taken out by the Iraqis, which was the reason they could not be contacted. If that was the case, what would be awaiting our arrival at Dhahran itself?

'It was an exceedingly tense time heading into the unknown and out of radio contact for so long, until contact was eventually made with a USAF C-130 somewhere to the south and heading in the same direction who had had the same problem trying to contact any control agency. It was a relief to be talking to another aircraft, and when contact was finally made with Riyadh Control, all aircraft landed as planned at Dhahran.'

After a four-hour flight, the aircraft reached Dhahran at about midday and the first operational defensive counter air (DCA) sorties were flown just two hours later. 'Aircraft were parked in a neat line under sunshades, which was very convenient given the extreme heat of 49°C, but this left them vulnerable to attack', noted Wg Cdr Black. 'Aircrew initially shared the operational accommodation of No 29 Sqn RSAF [also equipped with Tornado F 3s] and used their Ops desk, flying clothing, offices and briefing rooms, before constructing their own portacabin Ops facility. This was achieved by an ever-resourceful Supply Officer who managed to requisition a yellow JCB crane from a Saudi compound, repaint it green overnight and reposition the portacabins the following day, ignoring all Saudi protests that the crane was theirs. The groundcrew had three portacabin complexes on the line about half a mile from the aircrew and about 200 yards from the aircraft. All accommodation was air conditioned and quite satisfactory. Domestic accommodation was in the BAe compounds vacated by the departure of their civilian families.

'The aircrew manned two shifts from 1200 hrs to 1200 hrs each day, with 12 crews on each shift and each squadron manning one shift. The groundcrew manned three shifts of eight hours, with squadron personnel primarily servicing their own aircraft. There was considerable mixing when required, however.

'The perceived threat concerned Iraq's considerable capabilities, particularly in respect to chemical warfare, and the immediate worry was an offensive against Saudi Arabia before any further build-up of allied forces. This caused serious tension, and the issue of small arms and NBC [Nuclear, Biological, Chemical] equipment took priority. Nobody moved without it, and even the Saudis and BAe civilians were desperate to be issued with it. As time went by and more and more US troops arrived, the likelihood of an Iraqi offensive looked less likely, and the original tension eased. Everyone was keen to receive intelligence updates, and an intelligence briefing was given at every shift changeover.

'The build-up of US troops was phenomenal, and something rarely witnessed before. There was a huge ramp next to our line which constantly had six C-141 and six C-5 transport aircraft unloading, with others queueing up on the taxiway to take their place. This went on day and night. They reputedly had 100,000 troops in country by 16 August, and were aiming for 500,000. This level of build-up continued for a further two weeks. The troops disembarked the aircraft, moved into a nearby hangar, and were later transported up-country. Not, however, before having the opportunity to purchase items from the temporary BX [base exchange] they had set up in the corner of said hangar. It was strange to see troops boarding their transports to move up-country in full combat gear carrying cameras, radios, baseball bats, footballs, tennis rackets and the like, all recently purchased from the BX.

'Flying operations had revealed a problem agreeing our Rules of Engagement [RoE] with the USAF/RSAF. Their rules allowed them to shoot anyone straying over the border, whereas the RAF remained limited by RoE that required a hostile act to be committed before engagement. There was a 24-hour hold on RAF flying operations, and until the issue was resolved the RAF flew on the more distant CAPs. Our RoE would at least assist any Iraqi defector deciding to fly his aircraft across the border, whereas the USAF/RSAF rules would not. The issue was soon resolved, and as Detachment Commander Gp Capt Peacock-Edwards put it "if you are placed in a position to engage an Iraqi aircraft, make sure that the wreckage falls on the Saudi side of the border".

'In addition to manning the CAPs, aircrew needed to maintain flying currency, and so four pairs of aircraft flew each day on training sorties. All these sorties were flown fully armed in Lima (2250-litre) drop tank fitment and lasted two hours unrefuelled. With no experience of low flying below 250 ft or low flying over the desert, clearance was given for F 3 crews to practise low flying down to 50 ft. Any pilot will tell you that flying that low is difficult and takes every bit of concentration, particularly over a featureless sandy desert. After one such sortie, Flt Lt Chris Taylor of No 5 Sqn proudly announced in the crew room that he had flown past a group of camels in the desert, and that he had taken film to prove it. Crews went to the cine room to witness the camels in the desert, and sure enough there they were centre frame. However, on closer inspection the camels turned out to be sheep – Lord knows how low he was to take film of sheep. He learnt about flying from that!

'Clearance was given to tank from the C-130, so sorties from 16 August onwards used a Hercules for AAR [air-to-air refuelling]. The CAPs were positioned just south of the Iraqi border, and two of them were manned permanently with a pair of aircraft on each CAP. The assets available to man the CAPs were 48 USAF F-15s, 20 RSAF F-15s, four RSAF Tornado F 3s and 12 RAF Tornado F 3s. The RSAF manned one CAP at all times, and the USAF and RAF did the rest. The USAF held four aircraft on QRA [Quick Reaction Alert] at five minutes' readiness, and if a CAP aircraft went unserviceable, QRA would be scrambled to replace it.

'Normal sortie length was four hours with AAR. Nations operated as pairs, with no mixed formations. Some CAPs were more than 300 nautical miles from base. Transit to and from CAP was at 3000 to 6000 ft over very barren desert. Getting through the US Patriot SAM belt around Dhahran was interesting, but otherwise the procedures were straightforward and simple, and deliberately so.'

By 16 August, five days after the arrival of the RAF Tornado F 3s in theatre, there had already been three border infringements by Iraqi Air Force (IrAF) aircraft. One, thought to be a MiG-25 'Foxbat', was five nautical miles south of the border flying at 35,000 ft and 650 knots, and the second, believed to be a Mirage F1EQ, also penetrated five nautical miles into Saudi airspace. Both aircraft turned away as soon as they were radar-locked by USAF F-15s. The third incident occurred at night-time, when a contact was declared hostile by AWACS and locked onto by a RSAF F-15 – it also turned away in time. Other air activity included reports by AWACS of Iraqi CAPs north of the border.

Coalition CAPs were defined by 30 nautical mile squares stretching from over the sea in mid-Gulf to the east, to a position some 300 nautical miles inland along the Iraqi border to the west. Transit time from Dhahran to the CAPs was about 30 minutes. There was also a 60 nautical mile buffer zone between the Iraqi border

This fully armed Tornado F 3 is carrying four Skyflash SuperTEMP AAMs, four AIM-9LI Sidewinder AAMs and 2250-litre underwing tanks. The AN/ALE-40 flare dispensers can be seen under the engine doors (*Tony Paxton*)

and the CAPs, but only a 30 nautical mile buffer between the CAPs and the Kuwaiti border. USAF and RSAF aircraft could enter the buffer zone right up to the border, but RAF aircraft entering the buffer zone had to remain ten nautical miles from the border. CAPs were controlled by USAF Boeing E-3 Sentry or US Navy Grumman E-2 Hawkeye aircraft. For operational sorties, the Tornado F 3s were configured with four AIM-9L and four Skyflash TEMP AAMs and carried 2250-litre underwing fuel tanks.

Initially, the lack of a secure radio made it difficult to communicate with the US fighters on parallel CAPs, but this issue was resolved with the temporary fitment of Havequick equipment.

The heat was stifling from about 0900 hrs to 1700 hrs each day, with high humidity. Wg Cdr Black personally experienced 54°C one day, although the normal temperature was about 45°C. Although buildings and vehicles were air conditioned, energy expenditure during the day had a rapidly debilitating effect. Operational Turn Rounds (OTRs) were practised in daytime in full NBC kit for both aircrew and groundcrew, with worrying results. Working slowly, the groundcrew managed to complete an OTR under the watchful eye of the medical officer, but the aircrew demonstrated serious problems with overheating. The groundcrew discovered that the black soles on their RAF issue working shoes and boots transmitted so much heat from the ground that they became unusable, so alternatives had to be found.

The heat also affected the radar and avionics systems, making them prone to overheating. The solution was to switch off the cockpit air conditioning on the ground to divert the cooling air to the avionics and crack open the canopy. As Sqn Ldr Jones noted, 'the very long taxi pattern at Dhahran, which often took ten to 15 minutes, meant that the aircrew were bathed in sweat by the time we reached the take-off point. It was a beautiful feeling when we were able to engage the air conditioning just before we commenced the pre-take-off checks.'

Despite having successfully demonstrated Britain's political resolve and the ability to deploy swiftly, it soon became obvious that the Tornado F 3 was woefully inadequate for the forthcoming conflict. In particular, the lack of defensive aids left them vulnerable, and poor radar performance limited the aircrafts' tactical effectiveness. However, work was underway in

A close up of the Phimat chaff pod, which was mounted on the starboard outer stub pylon in lieu of an AIM-9 (*Tony Paxton*)

Britain to correct these deficiencies, and over the next few weeks some 40 aircraft were modified to meet Operation *Granby* requirements – RB199-104 engines were fitted, the radars were brought up to Stage 1+ standard, with vastly improved performance, and Radar-Absorbent Material (RAM) tiles were applied to the engine air intakes in order to reduce the radar cross-section of the aircraft. In addition, a self-defence suite was introduced, incorporating AN/ALE-40 flare dispensers that were attached to the engine access doors under the fuselage and a Phimat chaff dispenser that was carried on a wing stub-pylon in lieu of one AIM-9.

The weapons capability was also improved with the introduction of the Skyflash SuperTEMP AAM, which had a 20 per cent increase in range and better capability against electronic countermeasures (ECM), and the AIM-9LI, which had a better seeker head with improved flare rejection. In the front cockpit, the original stick-top switches were replaced by an F/A-18-style arrangement, giving the pilot control over the weapons while retaining Hands On Throttle and Stick. This update also improved the Missile Management System to allow selection of the actual weapon required. Avionics updates included the permanent fitting of Havequick secure radios and a Mode 4 transponder. Unfortunately, a Mode 4 interrogator was not fitted, and it also proved impossible to fit an ECM jammer to the aeroplane within the timescale. Finally, an attempt was made to make the cockpits compatible with Night Vision Goggles (NVGs).

Meanwhile, at Leeming, Wg Cdr D R Hamilton, commanding No 11 Sqn, was given the task of forming a new unit, No 11 (Composite) Sqn, to take over the Tornado F 3 detachment at Dhahran on a more permanent basis. The new unit comprised three flights, each of nine crews and 110 groundcrew drawn from each of Nos 11, 23 and 25 Sqns. Each flight was led by a flight commander from the respective unit – Sqn Ldrs M Barnes from No 11 Sqn, T R Paxton from No 23 Sqn and I Howe from No 25 Sqn. For a brief period, the aircraft were grounded so that they could be modified, including the fitting of the RAM tiles. The crews were also able to use a simulator equipped with the latest modifications.

'On 15 August we were at a civilian facility on the airfield at Shoreham, in West Sussex', recalled Sqn Ldr Paxton. 'Inside, was a Tornado F 3 simulator with a new, improved, so called Stage 1 radar. We did two one-and-a-half-hour sessions and then returned to Leeming. At Shoreham it was a civilian establishment, and we asked how it was that they had a sim with a better radar than we had on the frontline? The guy running the show explained that we had been lucky, as the sim was for the RSAF but the Saudis had not yet constructed the building in which it was to be housed – that was why it was still at Shoreham!'

The composite squadron started to work up with the improved aircraft on 17 August, making the most of the short timescale allocated to it. Sortie profiles started with 1-v-1 intercepts and culminated in four-ships operating against four ground attack aircraft escorted by four fighters. Within each flight, flying was in constituted crews, enabling crewmates to get used to working together as a close-knit team. Wg Cdr Hamilton later wrote that 'although we had had limited time to operate with the upgrades, operationally, we would be at least as good as we were with the old standard and would improve each day that we operated with the new. The plan was finalised for us to deploy in three waves of four aircraft via Akrotiri, the first wave on 29 August, the second wave deploying a week later and the last on 16 September.'

The first four Stage 1+ Tornado F 3s arrived at Dhahran on 30 August, flown by crews from No 11 (C) Sqn. The RAM tiles proved to be troublesome in the heat encountered in Dhahran. Sqn Ldr Paxton remembered that 'August in Dhahran was pretty hot. During the first few sorties we were concerned about the length of the take-off roll – it seemed excessive. It turned out that despite the outside air temperature being around 40°C, above the runway surface it was nearer 50°C, and that was the air going down the intakes.'

Due to heat soak, some RAM tiles became loose or unstuck following a CAP sortie, and each intake had to be closely inspected and repaired where necessary. This was a time consuming and very uncomfortable task for the groundcrews involved, lengthening turnaround times. It was eventually overcome with improved glue and reducing outside air temperatures.

The first operational sortie by No 11 (C) Sqn was flown on 31 August. Wg Cdr Hamilton, with Flt Lt R A Hinchcliffe, and Flt Lt C Bulteel, with Sqn Ldr M Barnes, took the Nos 3 and 4 slots, respectively, in a CAP sortie led by Wg Cdr Black, with Sqn Ldr D Bennett. Over the next weeks, No 5 (C) Sqn progressively handed over to No 11 (C) Sqn. Six more Stage 1+ aircraft arrived at Dhahran on 16 September, although one jet, flown by Flt Lt D Archer and Sqn Ldr B Burgess, caused a small diplomatic drama when it diverted to the holy city of Medina after suffering an engine failure en route. The last of the original No 5 Sqn aircraft finally departed Dhahran nine days later, returning to Britain in a single eight-and-a-half-hour trip.

Tornado GR 1 ZD707/BK of No 14 Sqn at Brüggen was one of the aircraft deployed to Bahrain on 27 August 1990. The Tornado GR 1s had been swiftly repainted at Brüggen in an overall 'Desert Pink' camouflage (*Andy Glover*)

Aircraft of the Tornado GR 1 detachment at Muharraq airport, Bahrain, parked amongst the TriStars of the local flag-carrier Gulf Air (*Mike Lumb*)

The official announcement that a squadron of Tornado GR 1s would also deploy to the Gulf region had been made on 23 August. The aircraft would be provided by the RAFG squadrons, since their aircraft were fitted with the RB199-103 engine, which gave slightly more thrust than the -101 engines used by the aircraft based in Britain. Furthermore, unlike the Tornado F 3, the RAFG Tornado GR 1s had a mature electronic warfare (EW) suite, including the Skyshadow ECM jamming pod (which was mounted on the port outer wing pylon), the BOZ-107 chaff and flare dispenser (mounted on the starboard outer wing pylon) and the Marconi Radar Homing and Warning Receiver (RHWR).

The majority of the aircraft were to come from Brüggen, but the crisis had broken over the summer leave period so there was no complete squadron with enough experienced CR crews available as a single unit. The designated lead unit was No 14 Sqn, and its OC, Wg Cdr R V Morris, was made detachment commander. Twelve crews were required, of which No 14 Sqn could provide five-and-a-half, with the remainder coming from the most experienced crews across the Brüggen Wing.

A hasty work-up was initiated, primarily in order to get all 12 crews qualified in AAR. The first conversion sorties started on 8 August, with Flt Lt M J Murtagh as No 14 Sqn's only AAR instructor. His first convexee was Flt Lt S H Cockram, and because of a shortage of dual-control training aircraft, their first mission was in a 'strike' aircraft (i.e. with no controls in the rear cockpit). Flt Lt Cockram recalled that '"Murts" was our only AAR instructor [he had regularly performed tanking during his previous tour with Marham-based No 27 Sqn]. I recall he was simply superb, and always made me at ease when moving around and towards the tanker, but the TriStar (my first sortie) was awful – long hose, low wing, poor perspective and only taking fuel off the centre hose, so no ability to refuel two aircraft at a time. The Victor, on the other hand, had a shorter hose, high wing and wing pods as well as a fuselage-mounted hose, so it was much more flexible.' Cockram himself was almost immediately signed off as an AAR instructor, and by the time he had finished his own conversion he had already cleared another four navigators on the tanker.

Another AAR instructor quickly pressed into service was Sqn Ldr G C A Buckley, a flight commander on No 15 Sqn. 'One day I was leading a four-ship of Tornados on a low-level training sortie', he remembered, 'when a call on the emergency frequency was broadcast for my formation to recover to RAF Brüggen. This was quite extraordinary, and when we landed at Brüggen the reason was made clear. I was an AAR instructor during my time at the TWCU [Tornado Weapons Conversion Unit], and on that day I was the only qualified AAR instructor in RAFG. This made me quite an important asset for the AAR training of RAFG crews.

'I was ordered to conduct an AAR sortie with another pilot in a two-seater ["strike"] Tornado and qualify him as an instructor. We were then to each fly another sortie with a new pilot and qualify them. In this way there would be four AAR instructors in RAFG, and the whole of the Tornado GR 1 force could be trained in AAR techniques. I duly flew four Tornado sorties that day, prior to returning home to Laarbruch by car, shattered.'

In this way all the crews were swiftly tanker qualified and were ready to deploy to the Middle East by 25 August, both AAR and combat capable.

Meanwhile, the engineers at Brüggen had prepared 12 Tornado GR 1s for deployment to the Gulf region, including painting them in a 'desert pink' camouflage scheme. All 12 aircraft, led by Flt Lt Cockram and Wg Cdr Morris, left Brüggen for Akrotiri on 27 August in three four-ships, each supported by a tanker. The following day, pausing only to incur the displeasure of the Station Commander at Akrotiri by delivering a rousing 'beat up' as they left, they continued to Bahrain. Here, they were based at Muharraq under the command of Gp Capt R H Goodall, who had previously been the Station Commander at Brüggen. In Bahrain, the Brüggen crews were joined by another 12 crews and six aircraft from Marham. Almost immediately, four aircraft were loaded with JP233 and held at readiness to attack airfields in Kuwait.

In-theatre training for the Tornado GR 1 detachment started straight away, with extensive use being made of low flying areas in Saudi Arabia and Oman, as well as the King Fahd range (just to the south of Dhahran) and the Qarin range on Masirah Island. The crews also familiarised themselves with flying the aircraft at heavy weights, loaded with two JP233 canisters, the new larger 2250-litre fuel tanks and two AIM-9L Sidewinder missiles. However, carriage limitations for live weapons (they were designed to be carried once and dropped, rather than flown repeatedly) meant that each crew got only a limited exposure. The heavier weights were later simulated by carrying two 1500-litre drop tanks under the fuselage in lieu of weapons.

The heavy weight flying was not without incident. On 28 October Flt Lts T J Marsh and K A Smith suffered an engine failure while flying with two JP233s and discovered that they needed to use reheat on the other engine during the landing.

To an extent the routine training carried out in Nevada, involving operational low flying over the desert, was a good preparation for low flying in the Gulf region, and crews were soon very comfortable flying at operational heights. Crews also practised night flying, using the TFR. Previously, they had been restricted by peacetime rules to 500 ft, but they were now authorised to the lowest selectable height of 200 ft. During this

Sorry looking Tornado GR 1 ZA466 after Sqn Ldrs Ivor Walker and Bobby Anderson were forced to eject in the wake of the aircraft hitting the approach runway barrier at Tabuk which had been erroneously raised across their path during a night landing. This accident occurred on 18 October 1990 (*Stu Osborne*)

A US Marine Corps F/A-18A Hornet of VMFA-451 from Sheikh Isa air base formates on a No 11 (C) Sqn Tornado F 3 following the completion of a dissimilar air combat training exercise. Both aircraft are carrying live AAMs (*Tony Paxton*)

practice it was discovered that, rather worryingly, the TFR could not consistently detect some types of sand.

While the Tornado GR 1 crews got used to the new environment, the Tornado F 3 crews of No 11 (C) Sqn, which by now had become known as the 'Desert Eagles', continued operational flying as usual. At that point in the crisis, there was a real threat of a pre-emptive strike by the Iraqis. All crews were on 60-minute alert at all times, including when they were stood down, and the unit typically flew four four-ship CAP sorties each day. A spare aircraft was maintained at RS-30 (30-minute readiness), and the crew came to cockpit readiness whenever an operational sortie was due to be launched so that it could fill the gaps in the event of unserviceability.

On 22 September, six more aircraft were flown to Dhahran, bringing the total to 18 F 3s in theatre. Wg Cdr Hamilton explained that 'this allowed, nominally, six aircraft to be utilised for training, with the other 12 available for operational CAPs. The training sorties were flown in fully armed aircraft, the only change being they were fitted with the smaller 1500-litre drop tanks, which had a higher g-limit than the 2250-litre tanks used for CAP. However, on occasions, the 1500-litre-fitted aircraft were used on CAP, and this proved to be of little consequence as they were less "draggy" and required little additional fuel from the tanker over a four-to-five-hour sortie.'

The advantage of flying training sorties in fully armed aircraft was that aircrews never had to switch between live and training fits, and groundcrews were saved the extra work of unnecessary loading and unloading missiles. Opponents on these sorties included packages of up to ten RAF Tornado GR 1s, Jaguars or USAF F-4Gs, although mutual intercepts against Tornado F 3s were also carried out. In addition, Hamilton recalled that some 'sorties included highly dynamic dissimilar air combat exercises against the US Marine Corps F/A-18, as it had a similar performance to the Iraqi MiG-29. The Marines were excellent, flying Iraqi tactics, so that we could hone our skills.' On another training sortie flown on 8 November, the Tornados were pitted against a force of 26 USAF F-16s and four F-4Gs.

As a result of the mix of operational tasking and training sorties, the 'Desert Eagles' were flying more than 1000 hours a month, against a normal squadron flying task of 280 hours. More than anything else, this was a remarkable achievement by the engineering groundcrew, led by Sqn Ldr G Morgan.

The reality of the operational situation was brought home on 16 October when a Tornado F 3 on CAP picked up a contact in Iraq flying at high speed towards the border. It was an IrAF 'Foxbat'. The Tornados were instructed by the AWACS controller to arm their missiles and commit northwards, but as they did so, the MiG-25 turned away and no longer presented a threat. In analysing this incident, it was realised that because of the speeds involved and the proximity to the border, if the 'Foxbat' had been engaged and shot down, it would probably have fallen on Iraqi, rather than Saudi, soil. This would undoubtedly have sparked off an unwanted crisis at a time when a peaceful solution was still being sought to defuse tensions in the area. As a result, the CAP positions were withdrawn another 50 miles back from the border.

A month later, Sqn Ldr Paxton, flying with Flt Lt M Tetlow, was leading a night-time CAP;

'My nav said that he had two contacts approaching the border from the north. He called the AWACS and reported that we had contact on two slow movers heading south. He gave their position, and an American voice responded, "No you haven't". The nav repeated the details and the American replied, much more insistent now "NO YOU HAVEN'T!" That's when the penny dropped. We subsequently found out that they were our own special forces helicopters returning from a drop behind enemy lines.'

On the ground, plans were being drawn up for the employment of the Tornado GR 1 force in the increasingly inevitable war. Wg Cdr Morris and Flt Lts Cockram, N T Cookson (from No 14 Sqn) and L Fisher (from No 9 Sqn) were frequent visitors to both the aircraft carrier USS *John F Kennedy* (CV-67), sailing in the Red Sea, and the Bahraini air base at nearby Sheikh Isa. The latter was home to the 3rd Marine Air Wing and the F-4G *Wild Weasel* units from Spangdahlem, in Germany, and George AFB, in California. Here they planned the initial stages of the air campaign, which would follow the declaration of hostilities.

As one of the few assets with an anti-runway weapon, the RAF Tornado GR 1s were tasked against Iraqi airfields. In the case of the Muharraq-based aircraft, the target would be Tallil airfield, to the southwest of An Nasiriyah on the Euphrates. Rather than a near suicidal run along each runway, the plan was to fly across the airfields, using the JP233 to 'bottle up' the IrAF aircraft by cutting off the taxiway access from the hardened aircraft shelter (HAS) sites to create minimum operating strips that would be too short for the Iraqi jets to use.

Apart from their 'in-house' work-up sorties, RAF Tornados participated in a number of exercises, including *Shifting Sands*, operating with British forces in the United Arab Emirates, on 21 October and the huge *Imminent Thunder* in Saudi Arabia on 15 and 16 November. The latter exercise involved more than 1000 aircraft, as well as naval and ground forces, from the Coalition that had formed in the Gulf over the previous two months. On the two nights of the exercise, eight-ship formations of Tornado GR 1s from Bahrain were tasked with simulating JP233 attacks against the airfield at King Khalid Military City in Saudi Arabia. The exercise was intended as a 'final warning' to the Iraqis that the Coalition meant business, and it was also an opportunity for the foreign air forces to practise working together en masse.

Now that there was enough time to work up Tornado F 3 crews with Stage 1+ aircraft in a less hurried manner, No 29 Sqn at Coningsby

A pair of Tornado GR 1s flies through spectacular scenery while carrying out low-level training in both Saudi Arabia and Oman (*Stu Osborne*)

and No 43 Sqn at Leuchars spent the autumn months preparing for a deployment to the Gulf at the end of the year. Flt Lt Elliott recalled that once he was back at Coningsby at the end of August, he was informed 'almost straight away that we would be returning to Saudi for the hostilities themselves. The squadron was immediately focused on an operational work-up the likes of which none of us had experienced.

'New kit came flooding in, both for us and for the jets. As crews, we were given a quick and dirty introduction to NVG flying – the first time this kit had been used by a fighter. The jets were only partially modified, and yards of black sticky tape were required to make the cockpit even close to NVG compatible. "Ghoolie Chits" were issued for escape and evasion, as were gold sovereigns, all of which was very sobering.

'We were tasked to fly Air Combat Training (ACT) to a base height of 1000 ft above ground level – at which point the cows and sheep looked huge. We flew large force, eight-versus-many, DCA sorties in the North Sea Air Combat Instrumentation Range as a precursor to what the powers that be felt would be our war role. The most demanding profile we flew [was] full-on ACT wearing an AR5 [Aircrew respirator] – trying to fight the jet with only a postage stamp size of unfogged visor was a huge challenge.'

At Leuchars, Wg Cdr A D Moir, OC No 43 Sqn, commented that 'August and September were spent preparing and modifying aircraft, making them suitable for combined control operations in the Gulf as opposed to the mainly over-sea interceptor role to which we were accustomed at home.' The flying training at Leuchars mirrored that undertaken from Coningsby.

Meanwhile, in Germany, Sqn Ldr C J Coulls arrived at Brüggen in October on his posting to be the Weapons Leader on No 14 Sqn 'to find a fragmented organisation consisting mainly of new arrivals who were yet to complete a combat-ready work-up and were in no way equipped to deploy. The remains of Nos 9 and 14 Sqns had been amalgamated into a single entity, which had been – much to the disgust of OC No 9 Sqn, who had been left holding the fort – predictably renamed as "No 11½ Sqn".

'This was a frustrating period for all of us. The first-tour crews were naturally anxious to get on with their conversion to the frontline and the award of the all-important combat-ready status, and the more experienced were champing at the bit to get involved in the real business that was developing in the Gulf. There were very few aircraft available to us to keep things ticking along, and news from Bahrain was sparse. All in all, a deeply unsatisfactory state of affairs.'

Preparations were being made for a more permanent arrangement at Bahrain to replace the Brüggen-based crews who had flown out in August at relatively short notice. Responsibility for this was given to No 15 Sqn under the command of Wg Cdr J Broadbent. At the same time, the other Laarbruch squadrons were earmarked for deployment to the RSAF base at Tabuk, in northwestern Saudi Arabia. Across the Tornado GR 1 force that autumn, there was a frantic work-up as the RAFG units hastily carried out AAR conversions. Both RAFG and British-based squadrons also ensured that their CR crews were qualified in operational low flying (OLF) and were well-practised in weaponry and fighter evasion tactics.

Most squadrons also took the opportunity to divide crews into formally constituted four-ships. The expectation was that even if squadrons did not deploy en masse, the smallest units would be four-ships. In the event, this thinking was absolutely correct, and the fact that the four-ships had flown and worked together as a team over a prolonged period made it easier for them to slip seamlessly into operational flying.

One development in the summer of 1990 was the initial introduction into service of the Air Launched Anti-Radiation Missile (ALARM). This weapon was originally conceived as one part of a family of anti-radiation missiles that would provide the RAF with its own Suppression of Enemy Air Defences (SEAD) capability against the Warsaw Pact's integrated air defence system during the Cold War. The end of the latter might have marked the death knell of the project, but with the possibility of hostilities looming in the Middle East, the first of the new missiles were quickly despatched to Laarbruch. Flt Lt D W Bellamy, a navigator on No 20 Sqn, was amongst the first crews to be involved with the project. He recalled;

'Initially, No 15 Sqn was assigned the ALARM role, and ground training commenced in the late summer of 1990. Fortunately, an executive officer from No 20 Sqn had had the foresight to recommend that one senior crew from No 20 Sqn also attend the briefings just in case No 15 Sqn was deployed to Bahrain in the offensive counter air (OCA) role.

'The No 15 Sqn Weapons Leader commenced the ground training with a wise reminder about MoD [Ministry of Defence] procurement. "When you want a missile, you specify its requirements, MoD goes off and competes it then buys it, and industry goes away and umpteen years later comes back with a product saying it works as requested. Then it's put in front of you guys and the first thing you will say is 'ah, but can it peel pineapples?"'" A few days later, No 15 Sqn was deployed to Bahrain, leaving No 20 Sqn to try to "peel pineapples".

'As a pre-production weapon system, there was no published concept of operations for ALARM, no flight reference cards, and nor were there any ground procedures. In addition, the only release-to-service authorisation originated from test firings conducted by the OEU [Operational Evaluation Unit], with the ALARM carried on the inboard underwing pylons. This meant initial ALARM training flights were conducted with centreline fuel tanks, which gave some interesting handling characteristics, particularly during AAR or flying at OLF altitudes.

'For the navigators, training focused on the mission planning and ground preparation stages of transferring target information, emitter libraries and launch modes from planning consoles to the aircraft using equipment referred to by the manufacturer by obtuse acronyms such as the HUSKY and PUGS.

'As a stand-off, fire-and-forget missile, ALARM endowed the RAF and the Tornado with a radical new capability. It could be launched at considerable stand-off ranges, climbing to high altitude before commencing its descent, giving a window of cover for specified radar targets programmed into the emitter library. Fundamentally, there was a choice between targets of known location and area suppression modes, with a trade-off between launch range (maximum and minimum) and the window of cover. Add to this the fact that ALARM could hit any of a number of radars within its library, No 20 Sqn crews came to realise that they could fire a "smart" missile and not know where it was going or what "pineapples it would peel".'

The changeover of Tornado GR 1 personnel at Bahrain started in November, with the No 15 Sqn crews' deployment staggered over a three-week period to allow a smooth handover between units. While there might have been some disappointment amongst the Brüggen crews at the possibility of missing out on some real action, the overwhelming feeling for most of the personnel returning to Germany was one of relief that they were getting back home to some form of normality. A number of them also believed that they might not actually be missing much, suspecting that the crisis would blow over without any fighting. By the beginning of December, No 15 Sqn was fully settled into Bahrain, with 12 CR crews divided into three constituted four-ships.

Nearly 900 miles due west of them, another detachment of 12 Tornado GR 1 crews, led by No 16 Sqn under Wg Cdr I Travers-Smith, had already arrived in theatre at Tabuk. Most of the preparatory work at the airfield had been done by Sqn Ldr J W Crowley and Flt Lt A M Randall from No 27 Sqn, who had moved across from Bahrain in early October.

Tornado GR 1 ZA470, originally from No 16 Sqn, was photographed during a low-level training sortie. The aircraft is configured with 2250-litre tanks, which had originally been procured for the Tornado F 3 force (*Mike Lumb*)

In contrast to Bahrain, where personnel enjoyed the luxury of the Sheraton Hotel, the accommodation at Tabuk was very basic. 'We lived in "suitable" on-base accommodation and had little help from the Saudi Base Commander (a Saudi Prince), or his staff, in establishing a Tornado operating base', reflected Sqn Ldr Crowley. 'Our working "accommodation" was a tent, a single power point and plenty of sand! Meetings with the prince were hard to come by, strictly formal and, at best, frustrating. Saudi facilities (operation centre, admin block, empty HAS site etc.) were strictly out-of-bounds to the RAF. However, progress was made, mainly due to much initiative and non-adherence to Saudi rules/guidance. Despite our frustrations, the arrival of a REME [Royal Electrical and Mechanical Engineers] party saw ISO containers transformed into an operations block, and numerous tents were erected ready for the arrival of aircrew.' Eventually, Tabuk would become the largest of the Tornado GR 1 detachments, with 19 aircraft and 30 crews.

Meanwhile, at Brüggen, Wg Cdr J J Witts, OC No 31 Sqn, had been informed in early November that he would lead a third Tornado GR 1 wing that would fly from the RSAF base at Dhahran, just across the causeway that linked Saudi Arabia with Bahrain. Like the other Tornado GR 1 detachments in-theatre at the time, this wing would comprise 12 aircraft and 24 crews. Half of the latter would be from No 31 Sqn and the other half would be provided by the remaining Brüggen units. Sqn Ldr Coulls recalled;

'News [of the new wing] certainly gave No 11½ Sqn a new sense of purpose, and we set about putting the limited assets available to us to the best use we could. The priorities for training quickly became clear, based on what we could glean from our colleagues in-theatre. The first challenge was to qualify everybody in day and night AAR, a skill that was not normally practised by Germany-based crews. The next priorities were to re-qualify all crews in day OLF. Finally, we also tried to give as many crews as possible some experience of medium-level bombing, from altitudes above 15,000 ft. Again, this was a skill that was not a normal part of the Tornado GR 1 force's repertoire, almost to the point of dogma. We saw ourselves as a low-level air force – a view unquestionably based on our favoured Cold War tactics – and prided ourselves at being better at low flying than any of our allies.'

Events a few months later would prove Coulls' insistence on practising medium-level bombing to be prescient.

At Dhahran, Wg Cdr Moir had arrived on 7 December to take over command of the Tornado F 3 detachment from Wg Cdr Hamilton. A week later, he had completed the handover, and on 21 December the final replacements took place with the arrival of the No 29 Sqn contingent.

Tornado F 3s tank from a VC10K from No 101 Sqn as they transit to their CAP position. The aircraft are carrying 1500-litre underwing tanks, as the 2250-litre tanks were needed by the Tornado GR 1 detachments. No 101 Sqn operated four VC10Ks from Riyadh in support of Coalition aircraft during the campaign (*Tony Paxton*)

Infra-red countermeasure flares are dispensed from the AN/ALE-40 fitted under a Tornado F 3 (*Paul Lightbody*)

Unlike the previous approach of the 'Desert Eagles', which had operated as a single squadron, the new Tornado F 3 detachment was split into two distinct units, dividing the mission tasking equally between them. 'From the outset', explained Moir, 'our main tasks were maintaining CAPs along the southern Kuwait/Iraqi border with Saudi Arabia and protecting the AWACS from possible fighter attack. Initially, we managed to achieve a limited amount of training as well, but this diminished as tensions increased, and by early January 1991 our efforts were entirely directed at operational flying.

'In essence, our tasks prior to the outbreak of hostilities were much the same as during the war, for we [were] the first line of defence against any pre-emptive Iraqi attack. We shared this DCA role with Saudi, French and US fighters under a co-ordinated plan.'

Throughout a 24-hour period, two crews would first maintain two hours at RS-20, followed by two hours at cockpit readiness and then fly a four-hour CAP sortie. For Flt Lt J C W Ward, a pilot on No 43 Sqn, 'It was obvious that we would be working hard and have very long working days, and that was even before the start of hostilities. We tended to work a 14-hour day, with very little time off.' Flt Lt Elliott, now on his second deployment to Dhahran, added that 'DCA missions would pre-tank south of the CAP, mostly off a UK tanker – Tristar, VC10 or Victor, but occasionally off the nightmare that was a KC-135 with a boom-drogue adaptor (a clearance we all achieved prior to deployment). Every time we flew in daylight, we witnessed the huge build up in our own troops and the massive camps being bulldozed out of the desert. Occasionally, we were encouraged to "cheer up" the ground forces with a show of presence.'

The Tornado F 3 operations continued uninterrupted from Dhahran, despite the 'Desert Eagles' having to move sites on the airfield to make space for the incoming Tornado GR 1 detachment. The Tornado F 3s migrated across to a bare site, known as the Egyptian Dispersal, in early January 1991.

CHAPTER TWO

FIRST DAY OF CONFLICT

After a brief work-up, the Tornado GR 1 detachment commanded by Wg Cdr Witts deployed to Dhahran at the beginning of January 1991. The engineering groundcrews, drawn from across the Brüggen Wing, were led by Sqn Ldr L J T Hendry, No 31 Sqn's Senior Engineering Officer.

'The next major issue', continued Coulls, 'was to get ourselves tasked onto the Master Air Attack Plan, which was being prepared by a very secretive organisation in Riyadh under US leadership. As usual, the UK had excellent access to the planning process due to our position as "ally of choice", and we had people in key roles in the heart of the organisation. However, by this stage there were in excess of 3500 USAF, US Navy, US Marine Corps and US Army aircraft in-theatre, and the arrival of 12 more Tornados was not necessarily the biggest news in town.

'The political process had made us very late, albeit welcome, additions and we needed to find our way into a plan that had been under development for nearly six months. It transpired that, because of our late arrival, we had only been tasked for a single, night four-ship for the first three days of the campaign. This was extremely disappointing, if understandable, but there was a promise of expanding our participation, bringing it up to two eight-aircraft formations per day, one timed to be on target just after dusk and the second just before dawn.'

JP233-armed Tornado GR 1s ZD895/BF and ZD745/BM from the Dhahran Wing. The starboard outer wing pylon on each aircraft carries a BOZ-107 chaff and flare dispenser (*Andy Glover*)

Sqn Ldr Coulls also attended a meeting with the British Air Commander in the RAF facility;

'I recall that this meeting was not the happiest that I have ever attended. There was obviously some disagreement within the UK HQ about our role, rates of effort and weapons selection, amongst other things. One of the biggest bones of contention was the likelihood of a US move to medium-level operations, for which the Tornado GR 1 was not best equipped, at a relatively early stage after the Iraqi air defence system had been neutralised. There was a strong feeling from the operators that we should resist this, but the Commander's view was that we would not be given a choice and the options were stark – operate at medium-level or sit on the ground doing nothing. No prizes for guessing who won the argument!'

At Bahrain, Sqn Ldr N L Risdale had been involved in pre-planning the first three days' worth of operations from Bahrain. 'The first issue we had was concern about the overall viability of the task', he explained. 'JP233 was designed specifically with Warsaw Pact runways in mind. The weapon was optimised for a runway about 8000 ft long built on an average Northern European sub-soil, not desert sands. The attack software required very accurate navigation and aiming both for the approach to target and during the lengthy delivery phase. We were well versed in planning and executing these profiles in our routine training, but these were over familiar, very accurately mapped terrain with a plethora of radar significant navigation and aiming features. The Gulf scenario required us to transit with tankers for about one-and-a-half hours, prior to dropping to low-level over a "barren featureless desert", and of course the mapping radar was not brilliant at altitude.

'The boffins always told us to use JP233 in the along the runway mode, as their computer model showed that only one aircraft with a really accurate delivery would do the job – but to get that one aircraft into position, the plans had two eight-ships attacking and then repeating this about four hours later. We had one eight-ship attacking once, and most of the runways were nearer 12,000 ft [in length] and had usable parallel taxiways. Tallil effectively had four 12,000 ft runways.

Armourers at Dhahran load the front canister of a JP233 dispenser. This contained 215 HB876 anti-personnel mines designed to stop repair teams from clearing the damage caused by the SG357 cratering sub-munitions carried in the rear canister (*Les Hendry*)

'We were really concerned about our ability to produce the accuracy that we would need for these missions to be anything close to successful. We came to the conclusion that the best we could do would be to "harass" the airfield's operations by primarily relying on the area-denial sub-munitions, and if the crater sub-munitions damaged some of the operating strips, it might stretch their recovery teams. Given all this, we came up with a plan to cut across the HAS site access taxiways and then spread four other short patterns over the runways/taxiways.'

Both detachments at Bahrain and Tabuk were boosted by last-minute reinforcements from the Marham-based Tornado GR 1 squadrons, with eight crews being sent to each location. The last part of the Tornado GR 1 force into theatre was a small detachment of reconnaissance aircraft under the command of Wg Cdr G L Torpy. The four Tornado GR 1As arrived at Dhahran on 15 January, with crews drawn from both Nos 13 and 2 Sqns. At Leeming, work-up training continued so that the Tornado F 3 detachment could also be reinforced if necessary, and replacement aircraft were ferried out from Britain. These nine-hour transit sorties took off in the dark at 0530 hrs and landed in the dark in Saudi Arabia at 1730 hrs local time. 'Spending a whole day's worth of daylight strapped in a Tornado cockpit was, to say the least, surreal', commented Wg Cdr Hamilton, who led four aircraft directly from Leeming to Dhahran on 11 January. After minimum rest, the crews returned home the next day with aircraft that required servicing at Leeming.

The majority of the ALARM training took place in-theatre after No 20 Sqn crews deployed to Tabuk in October. It was only then that they received the operational software for the weapon. Two dedicated ALARM four-ships were formed – Alpha, led by Sqn Ldrs R I McAlpine and R A Pittaway, and Delta, led by Flt Lts T J Roche and Bellamy.

According to Flt Lt Bellamy, 'the transition to war phase allowed No 20 Sqn lead crews to identify additional constraints in the form of high-level jet streams that would affect ALARM loiter modes, as well as electronic intelligence that indicated how Iraqi air defence units varied the position of mobile radars used in area defence of airfields. This culminated in the decision to select Corridor Suppression mode as the preferred method of delivery. Although many solo, pair and four-ship ALARM profiles were practised before combat operations commenced, it was not until after the first missile was fired that integration with mission packages occurred.'

In November 1990, the UN Security Council had adopted Resolution 678, which gave Iraq a deadline of 15 January to withdraw from Kuwait or face military action. Unfortunately, despite some high-level diplomacy, by early January it seemed more than likely that the Resolution would be ignored by the Iraqis and that war was inevitable. With the deadline fast approaching, the three Tornado GR 1 wings continued with an intense training programme. It was during one typical training sortie that the first Tornado crew was lost on 13 January.

'The No 14 Sqn four-ship was programmed to fly a practise AAR trail south through Saudi Arabia and into Oman, leave the tanker using night/poor weather procedures, carry out a simulated attack and then return to Dhahran', recounted Sqn Ldr Coulls, who was leading the

A Tornado GR 1 from the Dhahran Wing banks away from the camera, displaying its twin JP233 canisters in the process. Most of the Tornado missions flown in the first days of the war carried out low-level attacks with JP233 (Chris Coulls)

formation. 'We had also planned to conduct some additional training events, including the use of flares at very low-level to test their effectiveness against infra-red AAMs in that environment. We had planned to conclude the sortie with a bit of light relief, involving a segment of valley flying in the northern part of Oman, before returning to the tanker for the trip home. We knew that this was to be our last training sortie and were feeling comfortable in the desert environment after four reasonably demanding trips in quick succession.

'Our No 3 (Flt Lts Gibson and Glover) unfortunately didn't manage to get airborne, but other than that the early part of the sortie went to plan. We rendezvoused with the tanker and made our drop-off point in Oman in good order. Having settled at low-level, we completed the exercise with the flares, and a few minutes later our No 2 started calling over the radio for the No 4 to check-in. After several attempts, with no reply, and still with no sign of the No 4, we spotted a large plume of black smoke several miles behind us. We immediately turned around and headed for the smoke.

'To our horror, we found a very obvious scrape across the desert floor several kilometres long, the smoke rapidly dispersing and numerous unrecognisable items of debris scattered along the line. There was no sign of parachutes or sounds of emergency beacons on the distress frequency. Tragically, Kieran's and Norman's aircraft had impacted the ground while travelling at about 500 knots, after which there was only ever going to be one result. Thereafter, our long years of training took over and we carried out the necessary immediate actions. We were eventually relieved on-scene by an RAF Nimrod from an Omani base, climbed to rejoin our tanker and made our way back to Dhahran.'

Flt Lts K J Duffy and N T Dent were killed instantly when their aircraft hit the ground during a hard turn at ultra low-level.

FIRST WAVE – BAHRAIN

On 15 January, the UN Security Council Resolution expired and the personnel at all three Tornado GR 1 detachments waited for the start of the war. When they arrived at work the next day, the Bahrain crews were told that the war would start that night. In the words of Flt Lt N J Heard, a No 15 Sqn pilot, 'our mission was to attack Tallil airfield, a large fighter base in southern Iraq, as part of the opening "counter air" strategy to gain air superiority. The plan was for eight Tornados to drop JP233 runway attack munitions from low-level across runways and taxiways at around 0400 hrs [on 17 January] – just before dawn. This was bread and butter to us – night low flying using TFR was our speciality, although tonight we would be down to 200 ft, rather than the peacetime limit of 500 ft – and we would be releasing weapons as well!

'After taking off from Bahrain Muharraq at around 0200 hrs, we would meet up with VC10 tankers to take on fuel, routing northwestwards in Saudi Arabian airspace for an hour or so before letting down to low-level, entering Iraqi airspace way out in the desert where we knew it would be quiet. Twenty minutes later we would hit Tallil as four pairs, with 30 seconds between pairs. We would then return to the tanker before heading back to Bahrain in what would be a four-hour trip.'

The mission would be part of a much larger coalition 'package' of aircraft that would also be attacking Tallil, as well as other Iraqi airfields, in a co-ordinated strike on the whole of the IrAF and its air defence infrastructure. Each package would be supported by SEAD assets provided by the USAF and US Navy – this would include EF-111 Raven and EA-6B Prowler electronic jamming aircraft and F-4G *Wild Weasels* tasked with taking out radar and missile systems with anti-radiation missiles. There would also be fighter sweeps to ensure that IrAF fighters could not interfere with the ground-attack packages.

Meanwhile, at Dhahran and Tabuk, more Tornado GR 1 crews prepared themselves for similar JP233 missions – the Dhahran Wing was tasked with sending four aircraft against Mudaysis airfield (halfway between An Najaf and Ar Rutbah) and the Tabuk Wing would send two formations of four Tornados each against the airfields at Al Asad (between Haditha and Ar Ramadi) and Al Taqaddum (near Fallujah).

Later that night, the Bahrain crews also headed out to their aeroplanes. 'It was an emotional time', admitted Sqn Ldr Buckley, who would be leading the rear four-ship with Sqn Ldr I D Teakle. 'How was the mission going to evolve? Were we all going to get back okay? Most importantly though, was I going to be able to carry out the attack successfully and not let the rest of the squadron down? We were issued with a revolver, a holster, a magazine of bullets and a pack of gold sovereigns, the idea being that if you were captured, there would be a reward to your capturers for taking you to safety in the form of another pack of gold sovereigns.'

In the No 2 position, Flt Lt Heard remembered that 'Rob Woods, my navigator, and I walked out to our aircraft with the other crews with more than a little anxiety, although tonight's mission had hardly come as a surprise. We climbed in and got the jet going, and we were able to sit and await taxi time, contemplating again about what we were about to unleash.'

The IrAF base at Al Asad was a target for the Tabuk Wing. JP233 tactics were designed for employment against small airfields with a single operating strip, but most Iraqi air bases were very large with multiple runways (*Lars Smith*)

Lining up on Bahrain's runway, Flt Lts Heard and Woods watched as Sqn Ldr Risdale and Wg Cdr J Broadbent in the lead aircraft lit their reheat and rolled down the runway. 'Ten seconds later we followed', continued Heard. 'The Tornado was heavy with eight tons of fuel and four tons of weaponry. We got airborne safely and I started easing in on the leader's navigation lights to take up my position on his wing – night close formation had become another newly-acquired skill in the last few months – and we headed for the tanker rendezvous point.

'We joined on the tanker's right wing. The leader slipped behind the left hose to refuel. I moved behind the right hose and stabilised in the usual position, around ten feet behind the basket. We were tanking a lot lower than usual – at around 12,000 ft – because of the warm temperatures and our heavy weight, so the basket could be quite unstable. However, all went well, and with a bit of power I moved in and plugged into the basket first time – always a satisfying result! Fuel flowed and we were quickly full, so we unplugged and moved to the left wing to watch the other two Tornados of the front four-ship take theirs. We were now able to relax a little as we proceeded up the tanker-trail. Rob tuned in the BBC World Service on the HF radio, which, surreally, was still playing its ordinary schedule – the world was still unaware that the Gulf War was about to start.'

Approaching the drop off point, the Tornado GR 1s filled their fuel tanks once more and then descended to low-level as they headed northwards towards the Iraqi border. The crews busied themselves setting up their EW equipment, arming their weapons and finally switching off all their external lights. 'I had now plugged in the TFR on autopilot', recalled Heard, 'and we dropped down to 1500 ft above the ground as I checked that the system was behaving itself. I then reset the minimum height in stages down to 200 ft, and the Tornado settled beautifully at 420 knots over the invisible Saudi desert. On my moving map display I noticed the border approaching, indicating SAUDI ARABIA on one side and IRAQ on the other. This was for real. I was just about to enter the airspace of a foreign country at high speed, low-level, with fully armed bombs, cannon and missiles. I was about to start a war. At any point the Iraqis were now entitled to defend themselves.

'As we crossed the border, all was remarkably quiet – it was only later in the war that I realised how uninhabited this area was. We were at 420 knots, 200 ft above the desert, on track, on time and on speed – all critical elements of night TFR operation. We routinely worked to timing tolerances of plus/minus five seconds. We were now on an AWACS frequency and we could hear occasional reassuring calls of "Picture Clear" from the controller, which meant that there was no Iraqi fighter activity. We started to see bursts of AAA [anti-aircraft artillery] fire in the distance, and we knew that the Iraqis were now awake and alerted, but all remained quiet in our area. We now had some ten minutes to go to Tallil.'

At the head of the formation, Sqn Ldr Risdale remarked to his navigator, Wg Cdr Broadbent, about the impressive AAA barrage out to the left of their track. 'I should have checked my map before opening my mouth', he later commented, 'because we were about to turn left and point at that target – Tallil airfield. The US Navy formation attacking before us from medium altitude had stirred up a furious response that continued unabated for the four minutes or so that we were approaching it, and throughout our eight-ships' attack.

'About 20 seconds out we engaged burners to get the speed up to about 520 knots, and then went over the target in max dry, with the speed washing back to about 480 knots. We all took the auto-pilot out just before the weapon release in case of any TF pull-ups. We aimed to deliver at about 180 ft rad alt [radar altitude]. The trim change on canister release was significant, and I had to push quite significantly to prevent ballooning too much, and then get the TF and auto-pilot back in.'

In the No 2 aircraft, Flt Lt Heard's experience was very similar;

'In my "10.30" position, I started to notice a large area of AAA, and was staggered at the amount and intensity of the fire. I had a brief thought of "I'm really glad we're not going there." Just then, we reached another turning point and the Tornado – still on autopilot – turned left onto its next programmed track and pointed right at the AAA. It was then that the horrible truth dawned on me – that was Tallil! We were at the back end of a large package attack against the airfield involving the USAF and US Navy, so the defences were up and running.

'I stared at the interlocking mesh of AAA and my mouth went completely dry. As far as I could see, there was no way through that AAA, such was the barrage of incredibly high-energy cannon fire. This was not the sort of stuff that would sew a neat "Hollywood" row of holes in the fuselage – any hit from these shells would blow us to bits. The only thing in our favour was that the RHWR was clear – the Iraqis were aware of our USAF anti-radar missile support aircraft, so were leaving their radars off and just hosing away. We were quite invisible in the darkness, but I could not see how they could miss us with that intense barrage.

'Rob was now in his attack routine, marking an offset position on the airfield with his radar and then making minor adjustments, which the jet followed. We entered the AAA, and I was astounded to see that we were still more than a minute away from weapon release. This would be a long minute. I watched a gun open up just below and to the right, perhaps just 100 yards away from us, but his fire went blindly straight up, and I was astounded at how I could hear nothing of the AAA – I was still in a warm, quiet Tornado cockpit! At last the time-to-go in my HUD was unwinding – less than a minute to go. 480 knots attack speed – the jet could only just manage that in dry power, but reheat was out of the question in the darkness, as I would become highly visible. Thirty seconds to go – 15 seconds to go. I disconnected the autopilot and held the Tornado straight and level at 200 ft radar altitude, easily achieved using the HUD – we knew the autopilot would not cope with weapon release well, so manual flight was required for the next few seconds. I noticed the leader's JP233 munitions detonating exactly on time, slightly ahead and to our left – the first indication that he was there at all.

'With five seconds to go, Rob and I called "Committing!" to each other, meaning we were both pressing the bomb release buttons – either button would do, but we did not want a cock-up now and fail to drop the bombs. The munitions started dispensing – a five-second rumble as 60 runway cratering bombs and more than 400 minelets were expended, followed by three large thumps as the canisters automatically fell away afterwards.

'With all that weight and drag gone, the Tornado leapt forward, and I quickly re-engaged the autopilot – that would mean I would not inadvertently fly into the ground in the excitement. Seconds later, we emerged from the cauldron of AAA to the north of Tallil and began our route back to the tanker rendezvous point. I looked back to try and watch my colleagues make their attacks, but with so much AAA, I could not make out other JP233 strikes.'

Closely following the first four-ship towards the target, Sqn Ldr Buckley could see 'two red lines five or six miles away going vertically upwards, and as we continued, we could see more of them with similar patterns standing out against the night sky. This was a huge barrage of AAA – there were large lines and small dots just shooting upwards, some looking like candle lights at the top. We learned later that the small dots and dashes going up in spirals were actually small arms fire and the larger lines were the heavier AAA. An optical illusion gave me the impression that the AAA was coming from the top of a hill, which would be a sensible place to put a AAA site, so I decided to turn the aircraft slightly to the right to avoid it, bearing in mind my No 2 was also on my right. However, no matter where I steered the aircraft, the target pointer showed the AAA barrage. The AAA was actually the target, and we were going to have to go straight through it.

'As we ran in to the target, I was getting all sorts of comforting remarks from Paddy [Sqn Ldr Teakle] – we were spot on, and all the marks were perfect. We tripped out the TFR and proceeded to the target. Attack speed was planned at 480 knots, which, at that all-up weight, meant the throttles were almost at max dry power. We were now flying right into a huge barrage of AAA, with blue and red lines flying past the cockpit.

'I had been taught right from the start of my frontline career on the Jaguar that if you encounter AAA go as low and as fast as you can, and so I flew lower until the rad alt stopped reading (which I knew to be at about 100 ft) and then levelled using the vertical speed indicator in the HUD. To ensure that self-damage doesn't occur when a bomb is released and explodes on impact with the ground, a minimum height must be flown to enable the bomb to arm. This height for the JP233 was 200 ft and, therefore, I needed to climb the aircraft to 200 ft before weapon release.

'As we reached the weapon release point, I eased the aeroplane up, dropping the runway denial weapons in the four JP233 canisters that came off with a machine gun-like noise, very similar to firing the guns. This was followed by three booms and bumps as the rear canisters dropped off separately, while the front pair went together. With all that weight and drag removed, the aeroplane just shot forward, almost with the same sensation as taking off. Everything had been planned at the aeroplane's mid-speed range, leaving us with sufficient speed flexibility, should we require it, but after weapon release we went to maximum speed just to get out of there. The noise and response of the aircraft to the sudden release of the weapon load was completely unexpected. Coupled with my desire to return to ultra-low-level, it really felt like we were going over the edge of a large roller-coaster.

'As soon as we had bomb release, I returned to 100 ft and put the aircraft in a hard-banked turn to the right to get out of all that hullaballoo. I was absolutely buzzing as I flew that target run and subsequent run-out, and have often thought that if I had been taken out of the cockpit there and then and strapped to a monitor, the results would have been extraordinary. On reflection, flying down to 100 ft was not the most sensible thing to do. There were occasions when, after JP233 weapon release, the aircraft's INS [inertial navigation system] would drop off-line and the systems revert to a very unstable secondary mode, which would make the HUD difficult to read. I didn't use that tactic again.

'It was only when we got past the target and were on our way out again that we had time to actually think about what we had done, going through all that AAA.'

A few minutes later, all members of the formation checked in, indicating that they had made it safely through the target area. Flt Lt Heard later admitted that 'the relief, not just for our own success and safety but for that of our colleagues, was massive'. After crossing the border back into Saudi Arabia, the formation climbed up, in Heard's words, 'to greet the beautiful sight of the VC10, faithfully waiting for us on its towline'. After refuelling once more, the eight Tornados headed southeastwards towards the sunrise for the hour's transit back to Bahrain.

FIRST WAVE – DHAHRAN

At Dhahran, Wg Cdr Witts and Flt Lt A J Smith led their four-ship out to the runway for a take-off time of 0200 hrs GMT. The formation climbed out and headed northwest for the tanker towlines. Unfortunately, during the transit, the No 3 aircraft suffered an ECM equipment failure and had to return to Dhahran, but the remaining three jets rendezvoused with two Victor tankers. After AAR, made all the more challenging by some quite severe turbulence in the tankers' height block, the aircraft descended to low-level as they headed towards the Iraqi border.

Two of the key personnel at Dhahran, Sqn Ldr Les Hendry, the Senior Engineering Officer for the Tornado GR 1 Dhahran Wing, and Wg Cdr Jerry Witts, the base's Tornado GR 1 Detachment Commander, pose in front of the artwork adorning ZD740/DA (*Les Hendry*)

'During the descent, I switched on the TFR and locked in the auto pilot', wrote Wg Cdr Witts. "'A J" was busy getting a last radar position fix before leaving friendly territory. He was fretting slightly because of the errors that had accumulated in his navigation system, and he had begun to suspect that our INS was not performing as well as it should. As we dropped towards the desert floor, the night became darker and darker. Cloud cover now obscured what little starlight there was, and it was impossible to see anything outside the cockpit, except the lights of our two formation colleagues in the distance. As we crossed the designated "lights off" line, even these small, comforting, signs disappeared from view.

'The terrain was relatively flat, with nothing showing on the radar-scope to interfere with our smooth progress. After a while we flashed across the international border and into Iraq itself. "A J" and I marked the moment by wishing each other luck, before returning to business. (*text continues on page 51*)

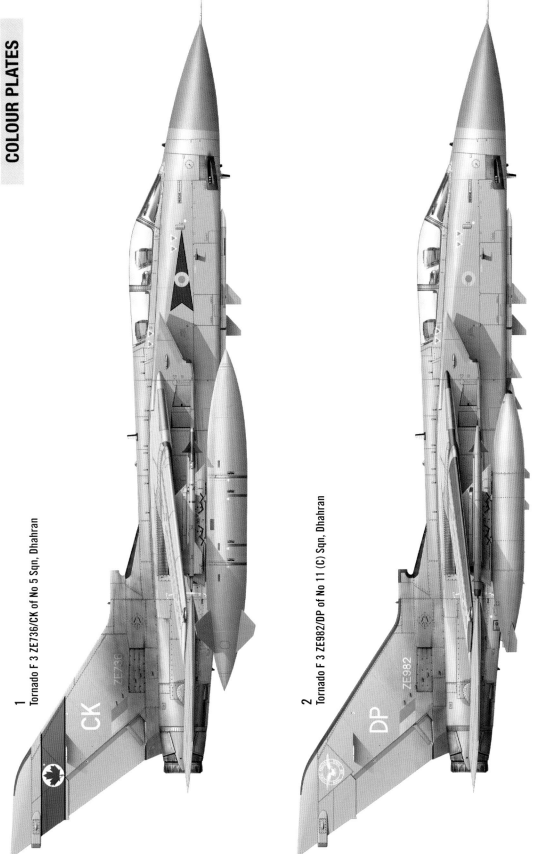

1
Tornado F 3 ZE736/CK of No 5 Sqn, Dhahran

2
Tornado F 3 ZE982/DP of No 11 (C) Sqn, Dhahran

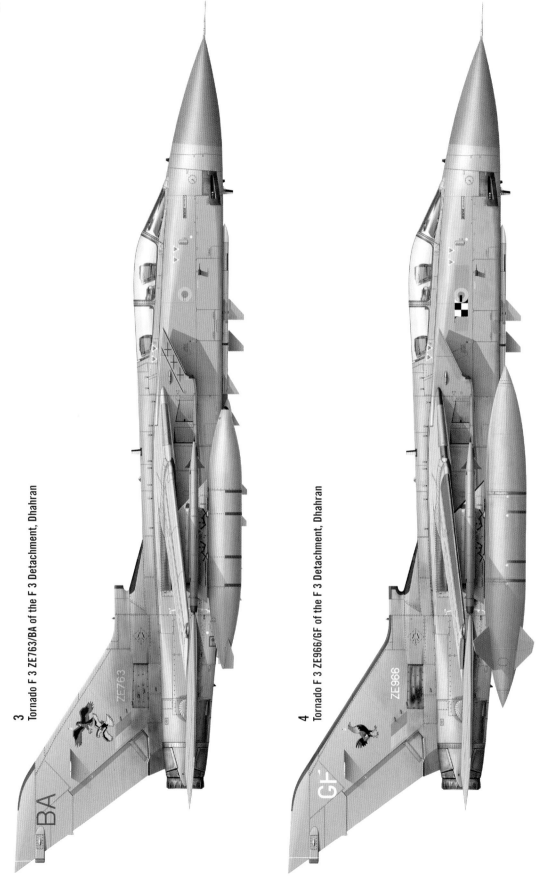

3
Tornado F 3 ZE763/BA of the F 3 Detachment, Dhahran

4
Tornado F 3 ZE966/GF of the F 3 Detachment, Dhahran

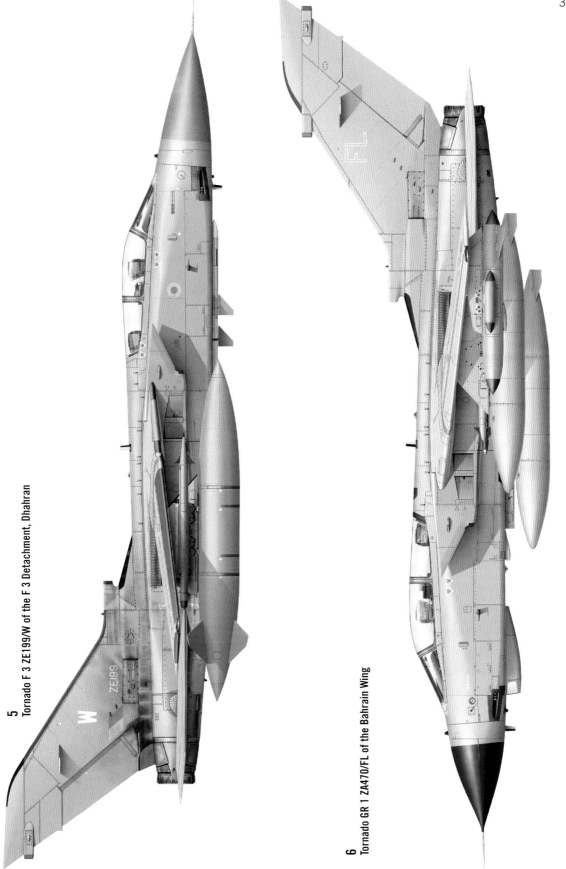

5
Tornado F 3 ZE199/W of the F 3 Detachment, Dhahran

6
Tornado GR 1 ZA470/FL of the Bahrain Wing

7
Tornado GR 1 ZD718/BH of the Dhahran Wing

8
Tornado GR 1 ZD845/AF *Angel Face* of the Tabuk Wing

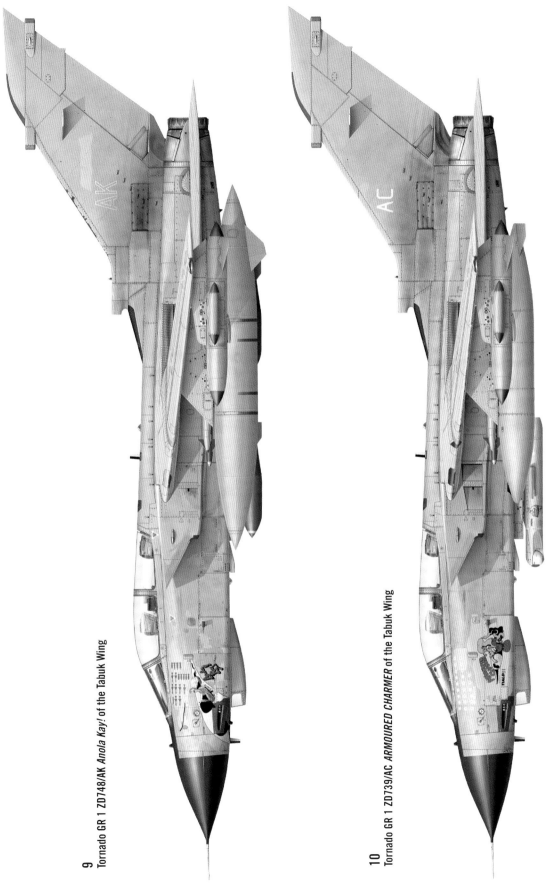

9
Tornado GR 1 ZD748/AK *Anola Kay!* of the Tabuk Wing

10
Tornado GR 1 ZD739/AC *ARMOURED CHARMER* of the Tabuk Wing

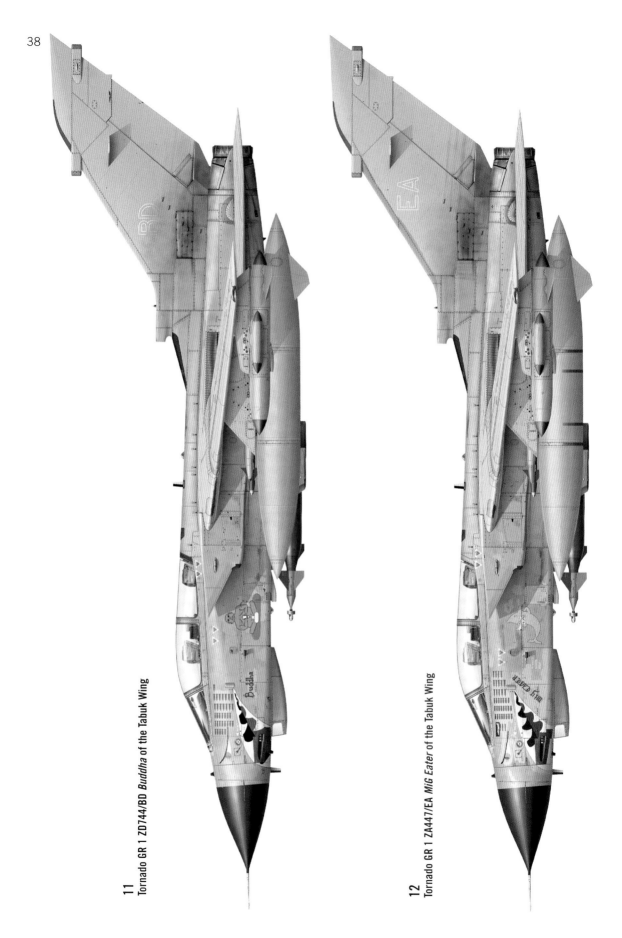

11
Tornado GR 1 ZD744/BD *Buddha* of the Tabuk Wing

12
Tornado GR 1 ZA447/EA *MiG Eater* of the Tabuk Wing

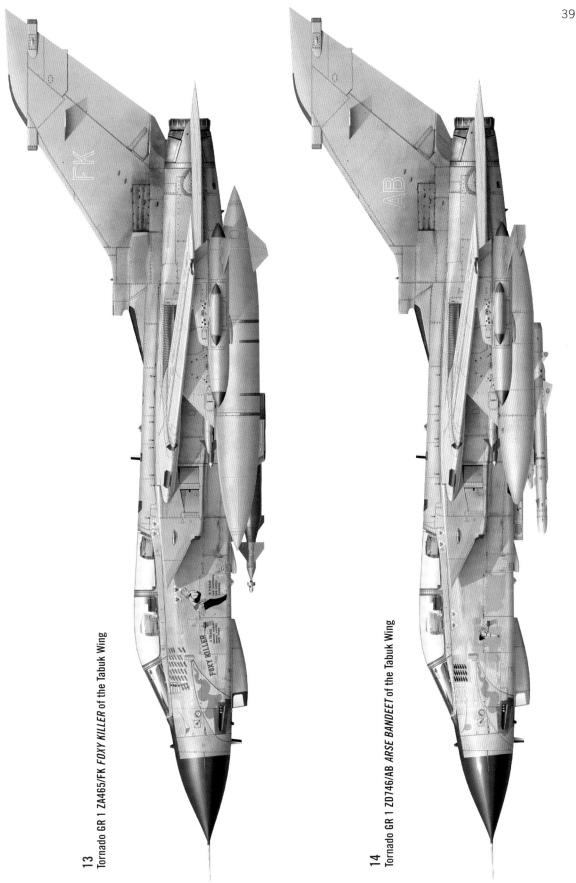

13
Tornado GR 1 ZA465/FK *FOXY KILLER* of the Tabuk Wing

14
Tornado GR 1 ZD746/AB *ARSE BANDEET* of the Tabuk Wing

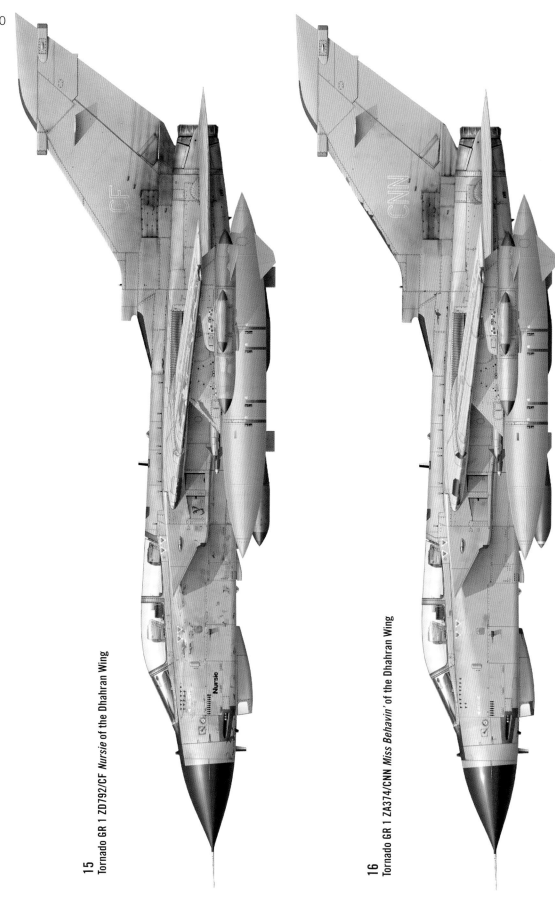

15
Tornado GR 1 ZD792/CF *Nursie* of the Dhahran Wing

16
Tornado GR 1 ZA374/CNN *Miss Behavin'* of the Dhahran Wing

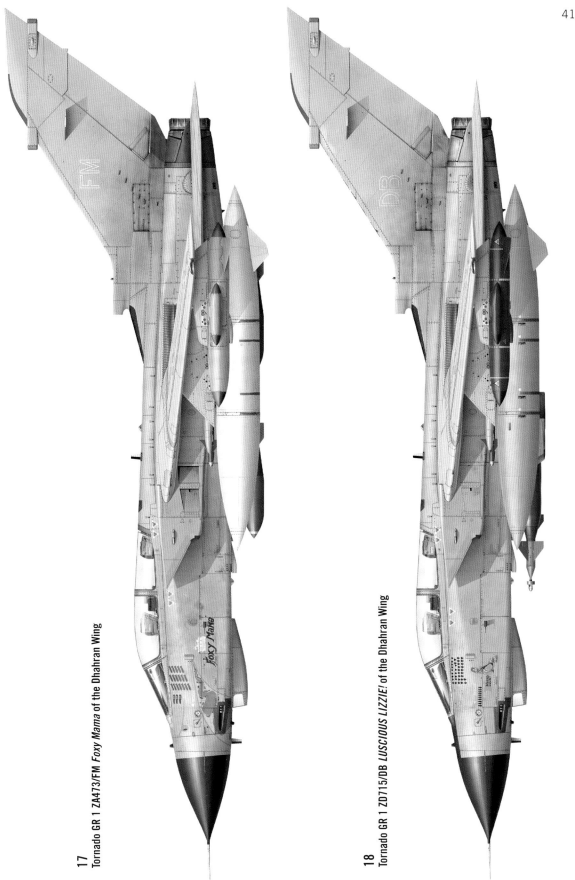

17
Tornado GR 1 ZA473/FM *Foxy Mama* of the Dhahran Wing

18
Tornado GR 1 ZD715/DB *LUSCIOUS LIZZIE!* of the Dhahran Wing

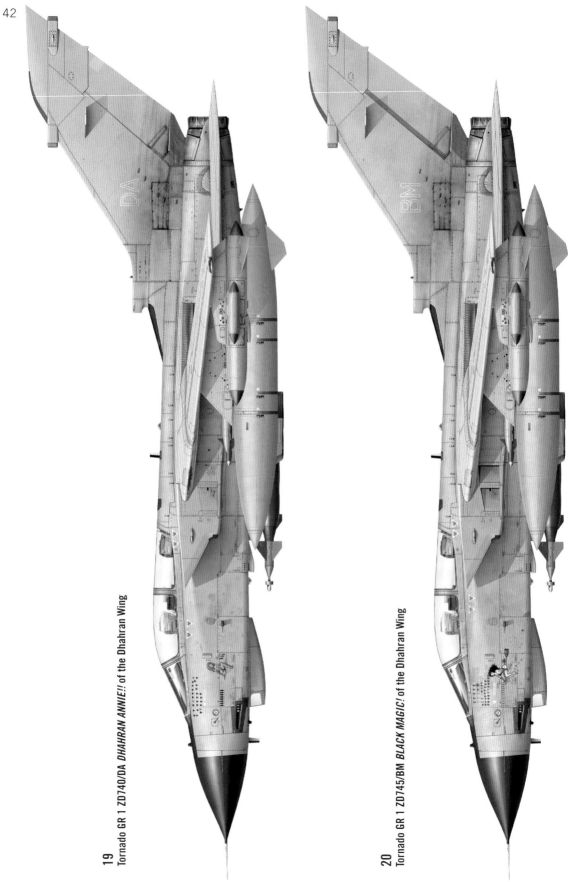

19
Tornado GR 1 ZD740/DA *DHAHRAN ANNIE!!* of the Dhahran Wing

20
Tornado GR 1 ZD745/BM *BLACK MAGIC!* of the Dhahran Wing

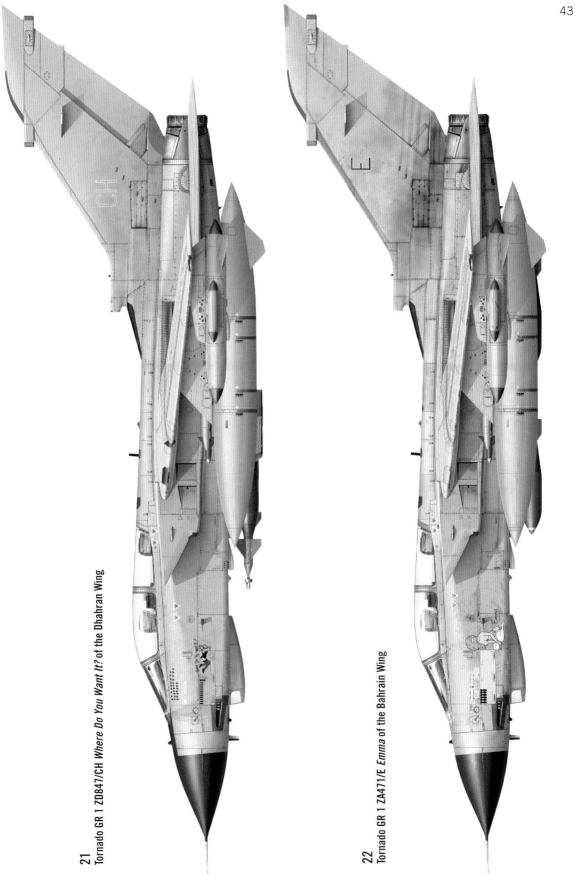

21
Tornado GR 1 ZD847/CH *Where Do You Want It?* of the Dhahran Wing

22
Tornado GR 1 ZA471/E *Emma* of the Bahrain Wing

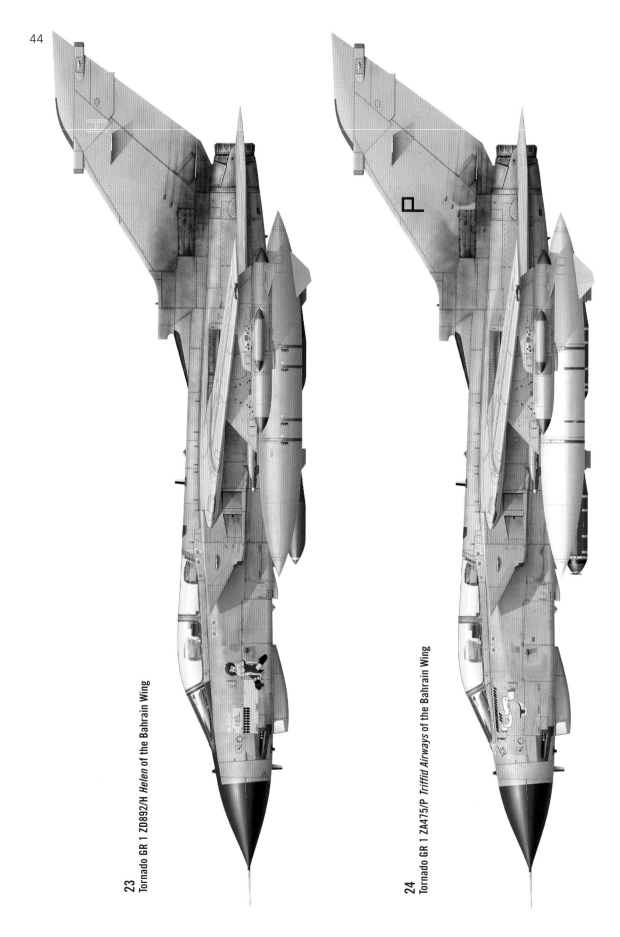

23
Tornado GR 1 ZD892/H *Helen* of the Bahrain Wing

24
Tornado GR 1 ZA475/P *Triffid Airways* of the Bahrain Wing

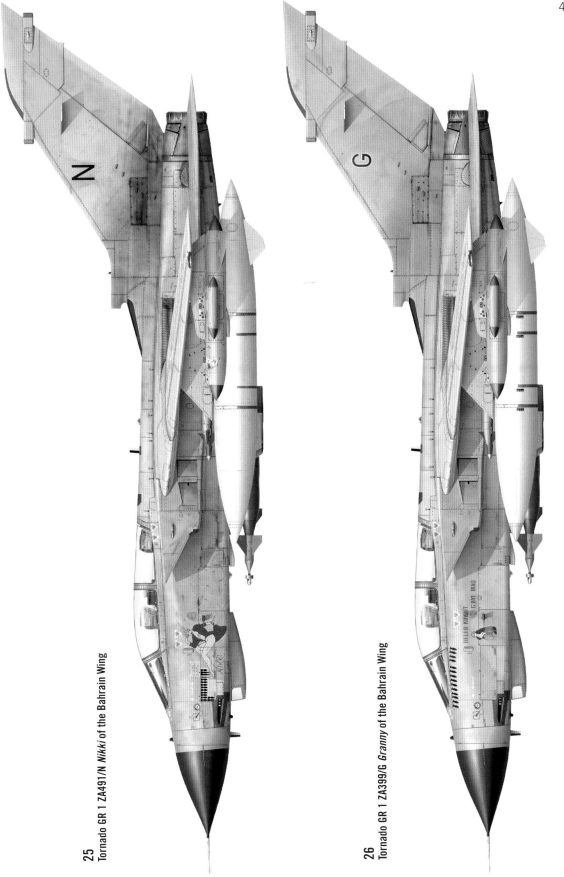

25
Tornado GR 1 ZA491/N *Nikki* of the Bahrain Wing

26
Tornado GR 1 ZA399/G *Granny* of the Bahrain Wing

27
Tornado GR 1A ZA371/C of the Reconnaissance Detachment, Dhahran Wing

28
Tornado GR 1A ZA372/E *Sally T.* of the Reconnaissance Detachment, Dhahran Wing

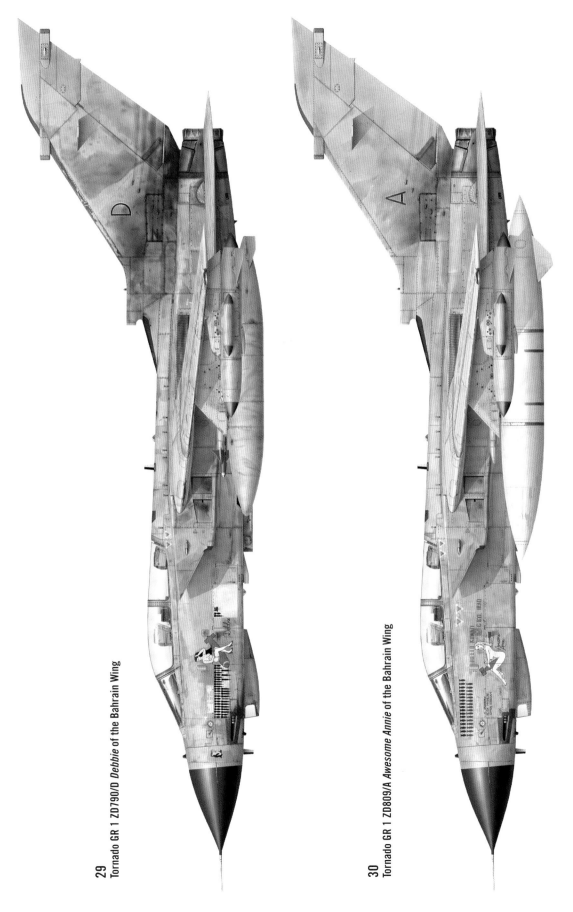

29
Tornado GR 1 ZD790/D *Debbie* of the Bahrain Wing

30
Tornado GR 1 ZD809/A *Awesome Annie* of the Bahrain Wing

UNIT BADGES AND NOSE ART

2
Tornado F 3 ZE982/DP of No 11 (C) Sqn,
Dhahran

3
Tornado F 3 ZE763/BA of the F 3
Detachment, Dhahran

4
Tornado F 3 ZE966/GF of the F 3
Detachment, Dhahran

8
Tornado GR 1 ZD845/AF
Angel Face of the Tabuk Wing

9
Tornado GR 1 ZD748/AK *Anola Kay!* of
the Tabuk Wing

10
Tornado GR 1 ZD739/AC *ARMOURED
CHARMER* of the Tabuk Wing

10
TIALD pod art *SANDRA* on ZD739/AC of
the Tabuk Wing

11
Tornado GR 1 ZD744/BD *Buddha* of the
Tabuk Wing

ado GR 1 ZA447/EA *MiG Eater* of
abuk Wing

13
Tornado GR 1 ZA465/FK *FOXY KILLER*
of the Tabuk Wing

14
Tornado GR 1 ZD746/AB *ARSE
BANDEET* of the Tabuk Wing

ado GR 1 ZA374/CNN *Miss
avin'* of the Dhahran Wing

18
Tornado GR 1 ZD715/DB *LUSCIOUS
LIZZIE!* of the Dhahran Wing

19
Tornado GR 1 ZD740/DA *DHAHRAN
ANNIE!!* of the Dhahran Wing

20
Tornado GR 1 ZD745/BM *BLACK
MAGIC!* of the Dhahran Wing

21
Tornado GR 1 ZD847/CH *Where Do You
Want It?* of the Dhahran Wing

50

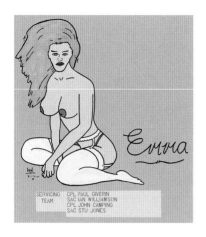

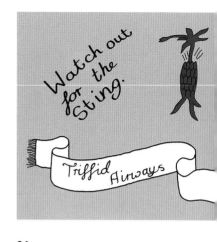

22
Tornado GR 1 ZA471/E *Emma* of the
Bahrain Wing

23
Tornado GR 1 ZD892/H *Helen* of the
Bahrain Wing

24
Tornado GR 1 ZA475/P *Triffid Airways*
of the Bahrain Wing

25
Tornado GR 1 ZA491/N *Nikki* of the
Bahrain Wing

26
Tornado GR 1 ZA399/G
Granny of the Bahrain Wing

29
Tornado GR 1 ZD790/D *Debbie* of the
Bahrain Wing

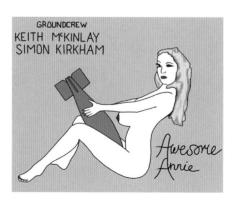

30
Tornado GR 1 ZD809/A *Awesome Annie*
of the Bahrain Wing

Our sortie had been fairly quiet until now. Suddenly, a faint "strobe" began to paint in the "one o'clock" position. As we sped towards it, the strobe became stronger and the RHWR computer annotated it as a "Fulcrum". My heart sank. The Russian-built MiG-29 "Fulcrum" was the Iraqi fighter that we feared the most. Although the Iraqi pilots were an unknown quantity, the "Fulcrum" was an agile high-performance fighter with a "look down–shoot down" capability. Here we were, ten minutes inside Iraq, and it looked as though one had shown up. We changed course slightly to the left and the strobe slowly moved around the clock on our right-hand side. Although there were no other threat indications and no warnings from the AWACS, the RHWR continued to insist that a MiG-29 "Fulcrum" was transitioning for a tail shot on us. There was nothing else we could do but sit and wait to see what happened. Thankfully, after a tense few minutes, the strobe faded and disappeared.

'I still couldn't see anything ahead, just darkness and the slowly unwinding circle in the fluorescent green HUD symbology that indicated time to weapon release. With about five miles to go, "A J" took one last look with the radar to make sure everything was spot on. It was, and I double-checked the last three switches, which would ensure that the JP233s would dispense automatically at the computer-calculated release point. This was really it then! For the first time in my life I was about to drop real weapons on a real enemy target with the intention of doing it as much harm as possible. I was tense but there was no fear. I was far more concerned that we had done everything possible to make the attack successful.

'"A J" counted down the seconds to release – "30, 20, 15, 10". I had a fleeting impression of a few shapes and lights on the ground ahead and, with about five seconds to go, I held down the commit button with my thumb. "A J" continued the countdown and, right on time, the aircraft started to vibrate rapidly as our two JP233s started to drop their loads. I could see a rapidly pulsing glow in my peripheral vision. I knew that the JPs would take several seconds to dispense fully, but it seemed to take forever. Suddenly, two massive thumps came from beneath the aircraft, so heavy that I thought for a second that we had been hit or flown into something. Simultaneously, various cockpit alarms sounded, warning lights flashed and the aircraft snapped into a sharp climb as the autopilot safety circuits took over control. As I struggled to get the aircraft back under control, I realised that the thumps must have been the empty JP233 canisters being jettisoned and that, somehow, this had caused the autopilot to drop out.

'Meanwhile, I could see all kinds of flashing lights and explosions going off outside the cockpit. "A J" was shouting at me to get the height down as AAA tracer arced over and around us. We very nearly hit the ground as I over-controlled the aircraft in my attempts to get the aircraft down too quickly. Now, I was frightened!'

As they re-crossed the Saudi border, it was clear that Witts' and Smith's INS had indeed wandered somewhat. Nevertheless, they still managed to locate the rest of their formation when the No 3 aircraft, by now in company with the post-strike VC10K, fired some flares to mark their position. Short of fuel by now, they caught up with the tanker and were able to top up for the last leg to Dhahran.

'It was wonderful to feel *terra firma* beneath the wheels again as we slowed down and taxied back to our dispersal', continued Witts. 'There, a large group of groundcrew were waiting to meet us, huge grins on their faces to match our own. We climbed out of our cockpits to congratulations all round. Jerry Gegg and Ian Long were immediately surrounded by the media pool and gave some memorable interviews for the TV and press. While we waited for them to finish, Les Hendry supervised the groundcrew as they stencilled the symbol of a palm tree beneath the cockpit rail of our aircraft. He planned that the aircraft should get one for each mission flown.'

FIRST WAVE – TABUK

The timings for the first formation attack from Tabuk were almost identical to those at Dhahran, with Wg Cdr Travers-Smith and Sqn Ldr J N Fradgley also taking off at the head of their four-ship just after 0200 hrs GMT. However, unlike the Tornado GR 1s from Bahrain and Dhahran, which had been supported entirely by American SEAD assets, the Tabuk Wing provided its own support in the form of two more Tornado GR 1s led by Flt Lts Roche and Bellamy, each armed with three ALARM. They would work in conjunction with two EA-6Bs (and their F-14 Tomcat escorts) that launched from a US Navy carrier sailing in the Red Sea to provide stand-off jamming to cover the Tornado bomber formation's approach to the target area.

Unfortunately, all was not going well in the No 4 aircraft, crewed by Flt Lt M Warren and Flg Off C M Craghill. 'We encountered technical problems with the stores management system during ground operations but had no time to run for a spare aircraft', Craghill explained. 'The problem meant that we would be able to dispense the runway cratering munitions from our JP233 runway denial weapon but not the mines designed to hamper clearance operations. With our aim being to put the runways at the massive Al Asad air base out of use – a daunting task with four aircraft, never mind three – we opted to go anyway. Sometimes these things cleared up once airborne.

'All ground ops were being undertaken in radio silence to maintain operational security, so at the appropriate time we moved out to join our four-ship and taxied to the holding point of Tabuk's military runway. The airfield in northwestern Saudi Arabia had two runways – one for civilian airline traffic and the other for Tabuk's resident RSAF F-5 fighters and their Coalition partners – primarily RAF Tornado GR 1 bombers and

Four Dhahran-based Tornado GR 1 aircrew photographed on the ramp shortly after their return from their first JP233 night mission. They are, from left to right, Flt Lt A J Smith, Wg Cdr Jerry Witts (OC No 31 Sqn) and Flt Lts Simon 'Shifty' Young and Adam Robinson (*Les Hendry*)

A pair of JP233-armed Tornado GR 1s are crewed up at Tabuk prior to the operational mission against Al Asad on 17 January 1991 (*Pete Batson*)

SEAD support for the Tabuk Wing was provided in-house using the British Aerospace ALARM missile. Tornado GR 1 ZD746/AB is armed with two such weapons (*David Bellamy*)

USAF F-15C fighters. As we waited in the darkness at the holding point, pre-take-off checks completed, an arriving airliner came up on the tower frequency and called for landing clearance. Air traffic control responded, "Cleared to land runway one three, traffic is four Tornados awaiting departure from runway zero six". So much for surprise.

'We received a green light from the tower and took to the runway for departure. One by one, we thundered down the runway and off into the clear desert night. It soon became obvious that not only would our stores management system not reset, the radar was also not working. As the formation flew to meet our tanker on the "Prune Trail" refuelling track, I tried everything I knew to coax it back to life but to no avail. With no radar we couldn't accurately update the aircraft navigation and weapon aiming system, making us a liability to the other formation members and decreasing our chances of an accurate strike on the runway at Al Asad. Right up to our turn to refuel we tried, but without the radar we were useless.

'We left the formation and reduced weight before returning to Tabuk, turning the broken jet over to the engineers to work their magic and get her ready for the next day. Mike and I sat quietly in the GR 1 operations room for the next few hours, playing chess and waiting for news of our formation. Eventually the radio burst into life, and three familiar voices checked in to report a successful mission and notify the groundcrew that they would be back on the ground in 15 minutes. A feeling of enormous relief washed over us both.'

Meanwhile, in the lead ALARM aircraft, Flt Lt Bellamy recounted that 'after AAR, we descended to 200 ft for a high-speed, low-level, penetration of Iraqi airspace. With the TFR system performing flawlessly, the aircraft passed close to Mudaysis airfield, where we could see Iraqi Mirages being towed into HASs.' As they pressed towards their target area at low-level, the ALARM crews also witnessed the first air-to-air kill of the war as an Iraqi aircraft tumbled in flames and crashed near their route.

Nearing Al Asad, the ALARM formation manoeuvred around an Iraqi

SA-8 SAM battery and then closed in on the target. Before firing, the pilots disconnected the autopilot and the navigators completed the ALARM attack routine. 'We fired off three ALARMs and two immediately plummeted to the deck. To say that was disappointing would be an understatement', reported Flt Lt Bellamy ruefully.

Tabuk's second four-ship was led by Sqn Ldrs G K S Lennox and K P Weeks, and it took off an hour after the first formation. Having refuelled from a VC10K, they entered Iraqi airspace at low-level and flew towards Al Taqaddum airfield. In the No 3 aircraft, Flt Lt J B Klein's two impressions of Al Taqaddum were of a 'heavy dome of AAA over the target' and the presence of Roland SAM systems. Despite these defences, all the Tornado GR 1s returned safely after a three-hour sortie, although only two of the aircraft claimed to have hit their targets successfully.

For the Tornado F 3 crews maintaining readiness 24 hours a day, there were long periods sat at cockpit readiness. Here, pilot Flt Lt Jerry Ward keeps up to date with the international news while navigator Capt Joe Lortie USAF listens in via the telebrief *(Paul Lightbody)*

On CAP to the south of Kuwait, Flt Lt Elliott recalled that 'turning hot towards Iraq, the airspace was completely empty. Turning cold towards Saudi, there were more contacts than we had ever seen.' However, the night was a relatively quiet one for the Tornado F 3 crews of No 29 Sqn maintaining the CAPs through the hours of darkness, although they reported vivid 'firework displays' over Kuwait from the SAMs and AAA firing at Coalition aircraft.

At both Tabuk and Dhahran there was a pause in Tornado GR 1 operations during daylight hours, during which the groundcrew serviced and re-armed the aircraft and the second shift of aircrews prepared for the night wave. This time the airfield at Al Asad would be revisited by an eight-ship from the Tabuk Wing. Meanwhile, the Dhahran Wing would send four more aircraft to Mudaysis airfield and another four to Wadi Al Khirr airfield. All of these missions would involve aircraft armed with JP233. Additionally, the Tabuk Wing would also mount a four-ship of ALARM aircraft to provide SEAD support for operations against H3 airfield.

Tornado F 3 DCA operations, however, continued through the day. The day-shift crews of No 43 Sqn took over from No 29 Sqn that morning, and Flt Lt Ward launched at 0800 hrs;

'We went north to the border, but only for an hour's patrol as all the tankers were being used by the bomber formations. So back to Dhahran again, quick refuel, staying in the aircraft, and off again for the second patrol.'

At that stage of the war, the IrAF was still expected to fight, and possibly to launch counterattacks against targets in Saudi Arabia, so the DCA CAPs were maintained around the clock. In later sorties, AAR was carried out from a TriStar tanker from No 216 Sqn, which had deployed to Riyadh specifically to support the Tornado F 3 detachment.

Despite the pause at the other two Tornado GR 1 bases and preparations for its own operations that evening, the Bahrain Wing was tasked to launch

Tornado GR 1 ZD744/BD from the Dhahran Wing armed with JP233 refuels from a Victor tanker of No 55 Sqn (*Andy Glover*)

four jets in daytime to harass operations at Ar Rumaylah airfield. The plan was for each aircraft to loft eight 1000-lb bombs into the HAS sites, this weapons fit having been chosen rather than JP233 so that the aircraft would not have to overfly the target in daylight. SEAD support would be provided by two EA-6Bs and 24 HARM-armed F/A-18s from the US Navy. One Tornado was unserviceable on start-up, leaving the remaining three aircraft to continue with the mission.

After taking off from Bahrain at 0430 hrs GMT, Sqn Ldrs P Mason and G Stapleton led their depleted formation westwards to join two Victor tankers, which refuelled the Tornados and dropped them off close to the Iraqi border. From here the formation followed a route that had been planned to avoid all known Iraqi military sites.

'The Tornados descended in escort formation to ultra-low-level in Saudi airspace and crossed the border with their radar altimeters unlocked', wrote Flt Lt M A C Paisey, who was flying the No 4 aircraft with Flt Lt M Toft. 'Evidence of earlier air strikes was visible from smoking EW sites [which had been attacked by AC-130 aircraft], and the formation proceeded to the target without detection. On the target run Nos 2 and 4 closed up on the leader, accelerating to 580 knots for the loft. At 22 seconds to go, the lead and No 4 pulled up, deploying chaff and flares on the southern track. During the manoeuvre 57 mm AAA fired at the aircraft, but both successfully returned to low-level, having delivered their ordnance on the target.

'No 2 pulled up behind the leader and No 4, but failed to release their stores. No 2 transmitted an unsuccessful attack, quickly followed by the fact that they had a left engine fire. The next transmission informed the lead that "we might have to get out". This was the last transmission, and occurred at a position approximately 15 nautical miles southwest of Jalibah airfield. No 4 passed the position on to AWACS while continuing to egress at low level with the leader.'

During the egress the remaining pair was locked up by SA-8 and Roland SAM systems, which they managed to defeat using a combination of chaff and low flying. The two Tornados rendezvoused with their tanker and then set off on the return leg to Bahrain, landing after a four-hour sortie. Meanwhile, it transpired that the No 2 jet, flown by Flt Lts J Peters and J Nichols, had been fatally hit by an Iraqi missile. After the aircraft became uncontrollable the crew managed to eject successfully, but were captured by Iraqi troops. As Flt Lt Paisey noted drily in his diary, 'despite the success of this mission, it served to bring home the reality of aerial warfare'.

CHAPTER THREE

COUNTER-AIR CAMPAIGN

On the evening of 17 January, Sqn Ldr P K Batson and Wg Cdr M C Heath led off four Tornado GR 1s from Tabuk to revisit the airfield at Al Asad. 'With the minimum of radio chatter, aircraft taxied at their designated time to arrive at the runway hold in the correct order for take-off at 2200 hrs Saudi time', recounted Batson. 'Departure from Tabuk involved a climb to medium-level en route to meet the Victor tanker in the nominated AAR area. The refuelling was all carried out in silence using light signals. It was a bit turbulent, and with the weight of the two JP233, it required much throttle pumping to get the aircraft to close on and stay in the basket. I could not recommend this technique as an AAR instructor, but it worked.

'There was no moon, so it was all a bit dark out and about, but there were some aircraft lights well below us. After refuelling, checks were completed in preparation for descending to low level and going "sausage side" – this involved switching all the external lights off and switching our EW equipment on. Once at 200 ft using the auto-TF, the aircraft was kept on course purely by the navigator keeping the "kit" in order. My job at this time was to change speed as ordered and monitor the TFR to ensure it was doing what it was supposed to.

'As we crossed the border, looking out the window all I saw was a lot of nothing, just varying amount of blackness. We overflew what appeared to be flaming aircraft wreckage at some point and saw something quite odd

The distinctive silhouette against the evening sky of a Tornado GR 1 in full reheat with wings fully swept. Most Tornado GR 1 missions during the first two weeks of operations were flown at night (*Stu Osborne*)

at several points along the route. As we crossed major roads, a spotlight parked on the road would illuminate, not aimed at us, just into the sky. It soon became apparent that it was a very basic but clever system of early warning. No doubt a conscript had been ordered to switch on the light if he heard an aircraft. The lights were quite well spaced along the road, and it gave a beam of light to the left of us and a beam of light to the right of us, forming a surreal corridor of our progression into Iraq.

'The closer we got to the target the faster we went, progressing in stages from 450 knots up to about 500 knots – the aircraft needed small bursts of reheat to overcome the drag effect of the JP233 at the latter speed. As the leader, we were at the front of the package attacking Al Asad. I thought that this could work in our favour, as we would be well over the airfield and out the other side before anyone knew we were there. The target area could be seen from about eight miles out – one minute's flying time – and all I saw was the lights of the airfield and the lights of an aircraft in the visual circuit. At this point I disengaged the autopilot to prevent the TFR giving pull-up commands and was flying manually.

'Mike and I rapidly discussed the threat the enemy aircraft could be to the rest of Dundee formation, so I attempted to lock my AAM onto it, but no reassuring growl came back. One of the disadvantages of using Air-to-Air mode when the weapon aiming system is in attack mode is that it cancels the latter, and that is exactly what happened.

'It was at about this time – 30 seconds out, and with no weapon steering in the HUD – that our presence was known to the enemy and the sky was filled with AAA tracer and bright white star shells exploding just above us. I manually selected pilot weapon aiming and moved my aircraft to ensure the munitions would go over the still lit runway. Out of the corner of my eye I spotted the aircraft that had been in the circuit rolling down the runway, so I adjusted the track and hit him as well. As the munitions deployed, the most satisfying sound I heard was the two weapon containers departing the aircraft with a "clunk, clunk".

'We were now in the middle of the inferno, where it was relatively clear of AAA, but we had to get out the other side. Off target, we visually sighted a missile launch so I manoeuvred the aircraft hard to the left to get on to our escape heading ASAP. It was at this point, flying manually at about 150 ft in a 60-degree turn to the left, that Mike shouted "roll left, turn left." I didn't really understand why he wanted me to increase the angle of bank, so I checked the artificial horizon and kept what I had, only to hear again "roll left, roll left." As I rolled out onto the escape heading and put the autopilot back in, all became clear. As I manoeuvred off target Mike had become disorientated with the stream of tracer around the cockpit and thought we were in a roll to the right, hence his urgent need for me to roll left. We left the target area at a now achievable speed of 520 knots, racing for the border.

'The gaggle set track for home, picking up their respective route and times to make the allocated exit gate to leave Iraqi airspace. At the border, the quietly ecstatic formation climbed to medium level and then we checked in on the radio – all present and correct with no losses, job well done!'

The SEAD support for the mission had been provided by another four Tornado GR 1s, each armed with three ALARMs, led by Sqn Ldrs McAlpine and Pittaway. 'All went well', remembered McAlpine. 'As we approached the firing point, I disengaged the auto pilot (200 ft auto-TF till then), raised the nose slightly and pulled the trigger to fire the missiles. Immediately, the ground below lit up from the very bright missile boost motors. Simultaneously, there was a shudder through the airframe as one-by-one the missiles left the under-fuselage stations. I recall thinking it was just like looking at Star Trek on the TV during a photon torpedo launch from the Starship Enterprise.

A close-up view of an ALARM, hung beneath a Tornado GR 1. The ALARM aircraft were operated exclusively by the Tabuk Wing (*Lars Smith*)

'As advertised, following a short period after launch, the missiles' red-coloured sustain motors lit and they entered their steep, slightly divergent, climbs to height. I admit to being a bit mesmerised by the display, and it was only when Dick Pittaway asked what the hell I was doing at 1500 ft that I sorted myself out and got us back down to 200 ft again. We didn't see any enemy defensive fire that night.'

As the Tabuk Wing was returning to base, two formations of Tornado GR 1s armed with JP233 were preparing to take off at Dhahran. Sqn Ldr G Whittingham and Flt Lt K J Baldwin were at the head of four aircraft tasked with attacking the airfield at Mudaysis, while Wg Cdr I Evans and Flt Lt R James were leading the second four-ship to Wadi Al Khirr.

'The planning and briefing were carried out without much bother, and when the time came to ready ourselves with our flying kit, sanitising our personal belongings, secreting our supply of gold sovereigns and walking to the aircraft, I remember the chatter subsiding', recalled Flt Lt W Grout, the navigator in the No 3 aircraft tasked against Mudaysis. 'We each seemed to withdraw into our own little world, thinking, "well this is it, years of training and now we have to do the real thing". In the cockpit, we both went about our checks as per normal. Our Skyshadow ECM pod was playing up, but that was situation normal. It passed the BITE (Built-In Test) and we taxied for take-off.

'We chatted a little about the prospect of going "sausage side", and what our tactics would be once across the border – lots of weaving and trying to spot missile launches. I started to recheck the Skyshadow pod and found that it would not cooperate at all. It was dead. We continued the sortie, with me trying everything to get it to work, but to no avail. As we approached the border, we discussed our next move. I was very adamant that we turn back. The words of the Boss echoed in my ear – "This is not a war worth dying for", "failed ECM is a no-go item, come what may". For me, the decision was made. It took a little persuading to get my pilot to return, but we did.

'There was silence in our cockpit as we returned to Dhahran (apart from compulsory R/T). We taxied back to the sunshades, shutdown, debriefed and waited in the crew room for our comrades to return. I felt remorse, guilt and worry that we had let the side down, despite the fact that our actions were fully supported. The wait was interminable, pacing around, unable to relax and feeling apprehensive. Several hours later, joy of joys, our team returned following a very successful mission – three pairs of JP233 on the runway and very little resistance. A huge sense of relief, followed by the usual banter of "what did you scrub for, wimps", or words to that effect.'

Theirs was not the only aircraft from Dhahran to suffer technical problems, as the No 4 aircraft crewed by Flt Lts P Reid and S Hadley had a generator failure. 'We approached the Iraqi border at 450 knots and 200 ft on the TFR, checks complete and as ready as we would ever be, running north towards the target', remembered Hadley. 'Then an amber caption went off in the front cockpit. The accompanying flicker of the TV tabs told me it was a generator problem. Sure enough, the right generator had failed. Resets worked only briefly, and so, just over a minute later and five miles short of the Iraqi border, we turned back. Our first war sortie was over. Or so we thought.

'In the climb-out we managed to contact the AWACS for the return home. Established in the climb at around 10,000 ft, suddenly everything went black in the cockpit. Everything. Black inside and out. It stayed black for a second, maybe less, before lights blared, attention-getters flashed and the "whoop-whoop" of the lyrebird warning tone kicked my senses back to life. We had experienced a momentary double-generator failure, except that's not what expected. It was certainly not like the simulator. Some of the kit was still working, but we had no time to ponder what had happened – we needed to land ASAP.' The crew diverted to the RSAF air base at Al Jouf.

In the second four-ship, both Wg Cdr Evans and Flt Lt James in the lead aircraft and the No 4 crew of Flt Lts G Harwell and M J Wintermeyer were

Armed with 1000-lb freefall bombs, a four-ship of Tornado GR 1s of the Bahrain Wing waits at the runway holding area, with their Victor tanker in the background (*Gordon Buckley*)

also having problems with TFR and autopilot systems, respectively – they too had to abort their sorties. Out of eight aircraft that launched from Dhahran that evening, only four made it to the targets.

At Bahrain, the evening wave consisted of two four-ships manned by crews from the Marham squadrons. They were tasked against the airfields at Shaibah, near Basra, and Al Jarrah, on the outskirts of Al Kut. The mission against Shaibah was led by Sqn Ldrs J Taylor and G E Thwaites. This formation attacked its target successfully, but unfortunately soon after making its attack, the No 3 aircraft, flown by Wg Cdr T N C Elsdon and Flt Lt R M Collier, hit the ground and both crew members were killed.

The second four-ship was led by Flt Lts G T W Beet and S Osborne. The No 3 aircraft had to return to Bahrain after the first AAR bracket when it suffered a GMR failure, leaving only three aircraft to press on to Al Jarrah. Shortly after crossing the border, the No 4 aircraft, flown by Flg Off N J W Ingle and Flt Lt P McKernan, was locked up and fired on by a Roland SAM. The pilot saw the missile in time to defeat it by manoeuvring and employing chaff.

Thanks to the efforts of the SEAD aircraft, the target was visible from about 30 miles away because of all the tracer from the AAA, which was firing blindly. As they approached the target area, the No 4 aircraft accelerated to the attack speed of 540 knots. Flt Lt McKernan described what happened next;

'About two-and-a-half miles from the target there was a loud "BANG" from the port wing and the aircraft, which Nige was now flying manually, pitched up to about 600 ft. I asked if he had any captions on his Central Warning Panel. He said "no", and I suggested that we get back down to a more comfortable height. It was very unnerving. I could busy myself with the radar and RHWR, but Nige had no such distractions, and I didn't envy him watching the orange glow turn into individual lines of tracer. As we crossed the airfield boundary, we both pressed our commit buttons, thus allowing the aircraft computer to commence dispensing the munitions at the right moment.

'Although we had been given some idea of what the next few seconds were going to be like, we were surprised by the effect of the JP233 system ejecting its munitions. It was like riding over a cobbled street in a cart with wooden wheels. The bang that accompanied the automatic jettison of the empty dispensers was a considerable surprise, despite the warnings we had received. Leaving the target was like going off-stage – we left the glow and ran into a wall of darkness. The AAA continued behind us until we lost sight of it.'

After an uneventful transit to the border, the crew climbed to rendezvous with the post-strike tanker. 'In all the excitement', continued McKernan, 'we had completely forgotten about the impact on our port wing just prior to the target. When Nige selected 25 degrees wing sweep, the aircraft became unstable, so he swept them back and we refuelled without much trouble with the wings swept at 45 degrees.' After landing using just mid-flap and without slats, the crew discovered that they had hit a large stork. As McKernan later commented, 'in the excitement of going to war, we had quite forgotten the everyday risk of a bird strike'.

With afterburner selected, Tornado GR 1s ZD790/D and ZD892/H from the Bahrain Wing get airborne from Muharraq (*Stu Osborne*)

At Bahrain, Flt Lt Heard reflected;

'We had just taken part in the largest air operation for decades, and the Gulf War was now definitely on. We could see that Iraq had taken a real pounding that night, and we wondered if they could sustain that for long. We had become combat-proven crews, and the change in attitude and confidence was clear, but by the time I flew my second mission – the next night – we had lost two Tornados, so we knew that it was going to be tough after all.'

The air war over Iraq and Kuwait was now in full swing. The strategic plan was for an intense air campaign to neutralise the Iraqi air defence system and establish air supremacy before moving on to systematically destroy the Iraqi military infrastructure and its support functions. For the RAF Tornado GR 1 force, this would mean, for the time being, continuing with low-level night-time JP233 attacks against the IrAF's main operating bases. 'There was no shortage of targets to hit', commented Flg Off Craghill, 'and the GR 1's early role was to keep the IrAF fighters and bombers on the ground where they could do no harm.'

However, despite the best efforts of Coalition ground-attack aircraft, the IrAF did fly during the first few days of the conflict, although they avoided combat. Flt Lt Ward reported that 'it was during those early days when we were on patrol that we got sight of the opposition on radar when they launched a few probing sorties up to the border. They must have been supported by a ground radar control because as we turned hot towards them, they just fled, so we didn't get within range.' Most of the targets that the Tornado F 3s were sent to identify were Coalition aircraft that had omitted to turn their IFF transponders back on as they returned from missions in Kuwait or Iraq. In Ward's view, 'it was really more a case of hustling the guys back in, rather than intercepting them, and making sure that they were all "friendly", and not just blips on the radar. Some of our more interesting sorties were at night when we flew with NVGs and we could see all the other aircraft going north and coming back in streams.'

Meanwhile, Flg Off Craghill was programmed to be in the No 4 aircraft for an attack on the massive airfield complex at H3 during the early hours of the morning of 18 January. The mission would be led by Wg Cdr Travers-Smith, with Sqn Ldr Fradgley, and would be supported by four ALARM aircraft led by Flt Lts Roche and Bellamy.

'Home to a mixed fleet of fighter and attack aircraft, H3 was defended by an aggressive mixture of SAMs and AAA', continued Craghill. 'Our objective was to sever access to the runways from the HAS dispersals at each corner of the airfield, which was thought to be easier to achieve than putting two runways out of action. In what would become a familiar pattern, we would have "area support" – fighters sweeping a wide area ahead of us for enemy aircraft, electronic attack aircraft jamming SAM radars and aeroplanes capable of shooting anti-radiation missiles at any radars which did threaten.

'These aircraft were not dedicated to our formation but knew where we would be at any given time to ensure they could protect us. Refuelling tankers loitered in the airspace of northern Saudi Arabia to ensure all aircraft had sufficient fuel to complete their sorties, and at least three AWACS aircraft fed information constantly to everyone through a series of daily changing radio frequencies.

'Once airborne, we checked in with AWACS on the western refuelling frequency and were guided to our tanker – usually a Victor – to take fuel during our northerly transit towards Iraq. Tonight, it was No 3's turn to have technical problems, so we departed the tanker as a three-ship. Up to this point we could see dozens of aircraft in the refuelling tracks, tanking with their lights on to minimise the risk of mid-air collisions. As we switched to the strike primary frequency and descended to low-level, we extinguished our lights, and so too did all the other aircraft heading into Iraq. Where once we had seen many, we now saw none. It felt lonely, but we knew we were far from alone. Our final radar fix before crossing into Iraq was a customs post at the Saudi-Iraqi border, which we streaked over at 200 ft, the TFR and autopilot adjusting our course as I updated the navigation and attack system.

'The run up to H3 was fairly short – we would be over the target less than 15 minutes after flying into Iraq. We crossed the border roughly parallel with, and only a few miles from, the Jordanian border, and already we could see sporadic bursts of tracer fire to our east. Word of our approach didn't take long to reach H3, and soon the airfield defences were active. SAM radars began to show on our RHWR and the AAA became more intense. We were in no doubt where our target was by now. Mike and I completed our pre-target checks and turned eastwards over the main Baghdad to Amman highway. Ahead of us, H3 was now alight with dense tracer fire up to around 4000 ft, and SAM radars were searching us out – indications of Roland and then Crotale on our RHWR as I dispensed chaff from our ECM suite.

'Two things happened more or less simultaneously now. A minute ahead of us, and eight miles closer to the target, our formation leader could see no way of prosecuting a successful attack due to the incredible concentration of AAA, and he called to the formation to abort the attack and egress west from the target area. As we began to turn, Mike and I heard the dreaded radar alarm from our RHWR, and I looked down to the computer display to see "SAM-8 target tracker" to our east. I turned on our jamming pod, dispensed chaff and called for Mike to roll out heading north. Almost immediately we were "spiked" again, and executed another 90-degree turn, overriding the TFR and climbing slightly to stay away from the flat desert floor a few hundred feet below us. Finally, with the threat seemingly negated, we turned south and re-engaged the TFR to get back down to 200 ft.

'We now had very little situational awareness on the other two GR 1s in our formation, but we knew we had to get rid of our weapons to ensure we had sufficient fuel to get back to Tabuk. As we rolled out south, a satellite airfield of H3 was directly on our nose about ten miles away. I quickly found it on the radar, Mike lined us up, and we prepared for weapon release. Right then what looked like gunfire erupted just off to our right, between our position and the Jordanian border. We had no time to react, and pressed home our attack. With the JP233 dispensed, the canisters fell away from the aircraft with an almighty thud, and we were able to quickly accelerate to 550 knots and run for the border. What we had taken to be ground fire had actually been the No 2 aircraft dispensing its JP233 around four miles to our west – we had somehow crossed paths in the confused egress from the target area.

'In a few minutes we had crossed safely back into Saudi Arabia and, turning our lights back on, were able to rejoin the formation for the transit back to Tabuk. For me and Mike, our first combat sortie had been about as busy as were able to cope with – but more was to come.'

Dhahran did not launch any attack missions that morning, but the base reacted to two air raid warnings in the early hours. 'This time the second was genuine', wrote the No 2 Sqn diarist. 'Many of us heard the explosion as one of Iraq's Scud missiles was successfully intercepted by a US Patriot missile.'

Just across the causeway from Dhahran, and also in the early hours, Sqn Ldr Risdale and Wg Cdr Broadbent led eight aircraft from Bahrain to Jalibah airfield. 'This time the target layout was about half of Tallil', explained Risdale, 'so just two long operating surfaces and HAS sites in each corner. I guess the target planners had decided that since it was smaller, we could attack it by ourselves, which after our experience with Tallil suited us fine. The original plan was basically a copy of the Tallil blueprint, with parallel track low-level ingress as an eight-ship gorilla, splitting into two four-ships to approach the target from two directions 90 degrees apart.

'Given our first night's experience we decided to close up the attack ToT [Time on Target] for each aircraft to try and get the whole attack done in as short a time as possible so as to minimise the threat from AAA. We decided to adapt the plan and keep six aircraft in one section, with just two – myself and Nick Heard – detaching from the front to fly a longer route and make the 90-degree cut 30 seconds after the other six had attacked. The first six were to attack essentially in pairs line abreast, but the angle of cut across the runways and ten seconds ToT separation between the individuals in

each pair, and 20 seconds between pairs, gave what we all considered to be adequate separation.'

Leading the rear four-ship once again, Sqn Ldr Buckley found this second mission to be 'much harder for us because we knew exactly what we were going to have to face. We decided to forget the medium speed rule and go in at full bore. The Tornado will go pretty fast when you need it, and once you get this train going with a bit of initial burner, not a lot stops it. This mission was a bit hairy because just beyond the airfield was an ammunition dump. The idea this time was for us to run through from south to north, turn left and left again and head straight back home. But because we'd decided to go "max-chat" (maximum speed), our turning circles were obviously going to be that much wider. Although we're briefed to compensate by tightening the turn, in the heat of the moment I forgot, as did the No 7 behind me.

'Running into the target, I looked out of the left side of the cockpit, and although I couldn't see an aircraft, I saw the unmistakable trail of a JP233 weapon exploding towards me. The aircraft that delivered that weapon must have only just passed behind me. We dropped our weapon, but this time I was ready for the kick in the back as the aircraft shook off its heavy load. I allowed the speed to stay high, which was a mistake because of the increased size of the forthcoming turning circle that was, this time, flown by the autopilot. Off the target, we had, in fact, to complete two 90-degree turns to achieve the run-out for home, with about a two-minute leg between turns.

'After the first turn, with autopilot in and TFR engaged, I looked in amazement at the target we had just attacked. The AAA was incessant and there were several explosions going off. But whilst I was exuding enthusiasm at the results of our efforts, a nasty event was brewing up for us. Suddenly, we were looking right into a fantastic fireworks display – we were right over the top of the ammunition dump, with AAA coming at us from all directions. The dump was heavily defended, and it seemed to be firing all of its weapons at once.'

On 18 January, Flt Lt M Stevens and Wg Cdr Moir were on CAP with another Tornado F 3 about 30 miles south of Kuwait when they were

Tornado F 3 ZE968/DJ heads out from Dhahran towards its CAP. DCA operations continued round the clock every day (*Tony Paxton*)

vectored north by AWACS to support friendly aircraft that were under attack. After jettisoning their external tanks and arming their missiles, both aircraft accelerated northwards towards the radar contact. 'Our US exchange pilot, Capt Brian "Hound" O'Connor, and Flt Lt Henry Paul were in the other F 3 slightly ahead of us and called a visual identification at about the same time as we saw three harassed A-10s making their way out of Kuwait', recalled Wg Cdr Moir. 'The pursuing aircraft [later found to be Iraqi Mirage F1Qs] had now turned back, and our radars showed them to be ten miles away. We chased them as far as we could without being dragged into the dense Iraqi SAM and AAA concentrations, but could not get within firing range.'

This incident also highlighted another limitation of the Tornado F 3 – the lack of a Mode 4 interrogator meant that the fighter was unable to declare radar contacts as hostile independently. As a result, the aircraft were constrained to remain within the coverage of AWACS, which could do so. This meant that, much to the frustration of the crews, they were unable to take part in OCA sweeps. They would remain on the defensive for the whole campaign.

'The less than stellar kinematic performance of the Tornado F 3' was another problem identified by Flt Lt Elliott, who pointed out that 'as the CAPs were close to the border, they were also therefore pretty much over the Iraqi [frontlines]. At best the F 3 could manage about 23,000 ft in dry power and "fullish" fuel, which left us feeling a bit vulnerable in daylight in particular. A lot of chaff and flares were expended and there was quite a lot of ducking, diving and running away.' Indeed, there were many occasions when the Tornado F 3s were engaged by Iraqi air defences while they were on CAP close to Kuwait. The aircraft were often fired on by AAA guns or locked up by SAM radars, and the lack of a self-protection jammer was keenly felt by the crews.

RECONNAISSANCE

The second day of the war also marked the first missions by the Tornado GR 1A reconnaissance detachment at Dhahran. There had been some speculation 24 hours earlier that the Air Headquarters intended to use the Tornado GR 1A to carry out bomb damage assessment (BDA) of the JP233 targets, but in the words of the diarist 'sense prevailed, and we weren't tasked'. However, on the evening of 18 January, two aircraft, crewed by Wg Cdr A Threadgould and Flt Lt T Robinson and Sqn Ldrs R F Garwood and J Hill, took off at 1900 hrs GMT and set off to search for Scud launchers.

'All had safe and successful sorties, which were achieved without tanker support using two 2250-litre tanks and two 1500-litre tanks per aircraft', recorded the No 2 Sqn diarist, 'but Wg Cdr Threadgould had a bit of excitement over the other side when, just before the target, it became clear that as the 1500-litre tanks were jettisoned, the 2250-litre tanks stopped feeding. Instead of having 4200 kg of useable fuel over the target, only 1700 kg was available. A quick dash to the border, followed by jettisoning of the big tanks and some super help from AWACS, resulted in a diversion to King Khalid military strip.' This mission pattern continued over the

next few evenings, with pairs of reconnaissance aircraft despatched over Iraq to search for Scud sites.

That evening, the Tabuk Wing attacked H2 airfield. In a change of tactics, only four Tornado GR 1s, led by Sqn Ldrs Lennox and Weeks, were armed with JP233, but they were supported by a six-aircraft SEAD formation led by Sqn Ldrs McAlpine and Pittaway – each of the latter jets carried a mixture of ALARM and 1000-lb bombs. 'For the first few nights of combat operations the AAA fire over Iraqi airfields was intense', explained Flt Lt Bellamy, 'and at times was seemingly initiated when an ALARM formation launched their missiles. For this reason, several ALARM packages changed their weapon loads to conventional 1000-lb bombs to attempt to suppress AAA sites and cut a path for other Tornados targeting airfield runways.' Although two of the SEAD formation dropped out through unserviceability, the tactic proved successful and all four of the JP233 aircraft were able to deliver their weapons on target.

Six more Tornado GR 1s, this time led by Flt Lts P A Fenlon-Smith and R L Hawkins, visited H2 the following evening. In another departure from the tactics of the previous two days, this time the aircraft were loaded with eight 1000-lb bombs to be lofted into the airfield.

On the same night, the Bahrain Wing revisited Tallil, which had been its target on the first day of the war. This time, like the Tabuk Wing, the Tornado GR 1s elected to provide their own SEAD support. Four aircraft led by Sqn Ldrs Taylor and Thwaites would each loft eight 1000-lb bombs onto the known AAA and SAM sites 40 seconds before the next four aircraft led by Flt Lts Beet and Osborne attacked the airfield with JP233. It was hoped that this tactic would shut down the AAA defences without providing them with the early warning that they had been given by the *Wild Weasels* on the previous night.

Tornado GR 1A ZA372/E rests between missions in the sun shelters at Dhahran. The reconnaissance aircraft were engaged in SCUD-hunting sorties in the western desert areas of Iraq (*Les Hendry*)

The No 3 pilot in the support package later wrote, 'I found myself tasked with targeting a Roland site on a SEAD mission – one of four aircraft targeting suspected air defences with four "slick" 1000-lb bombs, before eight far braver chaps were to follow through close behind and deliver JP233. The decision to perform "in-house" SEAD was primarily based on a lack of confidence in the SEAD that had been provided by US assets on earlier missions.

'Needless to say, this mobile system was more than four miles away from the location that had been provided by RAF Intelligence. We discovered this during the run in to the target when Bob and I had a Roland lock in our "two o'clock". The lock-up was shortly followed by a plume of white smoke going upwards in our "two o'clock" – and, to our annoyance, not moving left or right.

'After missile time of flight of less than three seconds, an explosion occurred that produced a silhouette of Dave and Robbie's Tornado. Bob suggested that some sort of evasion manoeuvre might be appropriate, so I duly obliged whilst he let off chaff, plus some flares that helped me to see terrain ahead, before the airfield batteries started firing such that night vision was no-longer an issue. Regrettably, quite a lot of speed had washed off as a result of the hard (reasonably level) manoeuvre and reversal back towards the target, plus it was now clear that our target was not underneath Bob's mark. The tracer above us resembled sheet lightning in daylight in the thin stratus. We pulled up into it to loft out bombs on what had once been a Roland battery, but what I guessed was now desert, before we focused on getting back to low level and getting home.'

Unfortunately, during this sortie, the aircraft of Flt Lts D J Waddington and R J Stewart was hit by a Roland missile. The crew managed to eject and were quickly captured by the Iraqis.

By 20 January the three Tornado GR 1 wings had begun to experiment with their own separate tactical approaches. At Tabuk, JP233 was

A pair of Tornado GR 1s from the Tabuk Wing armed with ALARM missiles refuel from a VC10K before crossing the Iraqi border (*David Bellamy*)

abandoned in favour of 1000-lb bombs delivered from lofted attacks. Although these weapons would not be effective against the operating surfaces, they would cause damage against other parts of the airfield infrastructure, including HASs. The six aircraft tasked against Ruwayshid airfield, close to the Jordanian border, in the early hours of the morning each lofted eight bombs onto the target.

At Bahrain, Sqn Ldr Buckley reported that 'we heard from another base that they had a reasonable amount of success lofting bombs with an airburst setting on the fuse. Our initial sorties adopted the tactic of going into the airfield target behind the Americans. Unfortunately, on the first two sorties, by the time we reached the target they were well and truly stirred up like a hornet's nest, with heavy AAA going off in all directions. It was better to be on our own with the first two aircraft loaded with JP233, the next four with 1000-lb bombs set for airburst and the last two with JP233, again, to run through the black holes that would be left. This was the tactic for the third sortie.'

'This mission was one of those trips where just about anything that could go wrong did go wrong', wrote Sqn Ldr Risdale afterwards. 'The No 8 aircraft (armed with JP233) went unserviceable on the ground, but the remainder got together, and we rendezvoused with the tankers for our first of two brackets. I was about three-quarters full when we flew into a big, bumpy, cumulonimbus cloud. Despite [selecting reheat] I dropped out, as did Nick on the other wing. We then spent some time bouncing up and down trying to synchronise the bounces with the hose! Nick "spoked", but I managed to get back in and fill, then Nick completed his refuelling on my hose. The rear tanker team was having similar problems.'

'This whole sortie was an absolute nightmare', agreed Sqn Ldr Buckley. 'The weather was bad, the two tankers wouldn't come out of the cloud, and trying to tank in cloud at night is bad news. One aeroplane

Tornado GR 1s ZD745/BM and ZA457/CE, each loaded with eight 1000-lb freefall bombs and 2250-litre underwing tanks, refuel from a VC10K tanker from No 101 Sqn (*Andy Glover*)

had to turn back as his fuel wouldn't transfer correctly and my No 2 just couldn't physically get his probe into the tanker's refuelling basket, so I had to send him home. Eventually, only four of us got to the target.

'When we left the tanker and dropped down to low-level, there was ground fog everywhere. So, once again, we found ourselves at 200 ft and 420 knots relying totally on the aircraft's systems. As we ran into our initial point for the attack, I could actually see the effect of the other aeroplanes' weapons, but the results were disappointing. The final run-in to this target was after a 90-degree turn onto the final attack heading, and so for some time I was flying along the perimeter of the airfield, with a good view of the attacks made by the rest of our lead formation.

'The idea of the loft attack was to suppress the AAA and create a hole into which the rear two of the formation could fly through unimpeded and drop their bombs. If the mission had gone ahead as planned, there would have been 32 1000-lb bombs air-bursting (literally) over the heads of the Iraqi forces that were throwing up the AAA. However, due to the unserviceability problems en route, there were only four aircraft now attacking the airfield.'

In the lead pair, Sqn Ldr Risdale was approaching the target and, in his words, 'looking forward to having a quiet JP233 attack, rather than flying through the flak firestorm. Unfortunately, the air defences at Al Jarrah must have been more sophisticated than the other airfields we had attacked because the AAA started up about 30 seconds before our arrival, and for a third time we went through on a wing and a prayer. But, of course, this was our third attack, and both of us were convinced that the barrage was more aimed and, consequently, more threatening. I was also convinced that my navigator John had selected "long stick", since I had the impression that I could feel every single sub-munition come out slowly, rather than the almost machine gun rattle I recalled from the first run. How the brain plays tricks!'

'The first two aircraft had run through as planned, delivering their JP233 weapons', continued Sqn Ldr Buckley. 'The next aircraft through, just ahead of my planned run, was a loft attack of eight 1000-lb bombs. The sight of these exploding mid-air was shocking to the senses, but amazingly the AAA did not diminish, and I realised that I was going to have to make the same attack into the maelstrom that was the target.

'I got the burners going until I had no more spare fuel left, so I shut them off, but then I didn't have the speed. Then the AAA started whistling past the canopy, and I told Paddy, "We're here, we're here", but he said we still had 50 seconds to go. At that stage I tripped out the TFR and just went on in. When I looked at the film afterwards, I'd actually allowed the aeroplane to climb to 600 ft. I thought this was suicidal, because all my teaching had been to go as low as possible when facing AAA. At least I had got some speed on.

'With the acceleration that the short burst of reheat gave me, we were now doing about 600 knots, but with the reheat out the speed started to wash off alarmingly. By the time I pulled up for the attack we were back to around 550 knots, which was more than enough for an attack *with* reheat, but without reheat to sustain the speed during the upwards manoeuvre, there was a chance the aircraft computer would not get a release solution and the bombs would not be released.

'The Iraqis had pushed the defence line of the airfield out to about three to four miles, which was right in the heart of the loft envelope. In effect, we were pulling up right into the teeth of the AAA. Fortunately, the bombs did release with an almost normal profile. At weapon release, the aircraft's pitch attitude was about 20 degrees at around 1500 ft. The idea is then to get the aircraft back down to low-level as quickly as possible whilst turning away from the target. This was a tricky manoeuvre at the best of times, but when executed at night, with AAA flying past the cockpit, the pressure of not having enough fuel to return home and the ever-present nightmare of disorientation, it was even more hazardous.

'Paddy realised we didn't have enough fuel to get home, so we jettisoned the twin store bomb carriers and "cleaned" the aeroplane. We got home all right, but upon walking into the debriefing room I met the pilot from the lead formation who had just carried out the same loft attack as me. "I don't have too many more of those inside me", he said, which came as quite a shock to me. He was the last person I expected to hear that sort of comment from. It made me assess my feelings. Although I felt as though I could continue for some time to come, it was apparent that something had to done about our tactics, and how they related to the incredible AAA barrages that we faced each time we went and attacked an airfield.

'The meeting to modify our tactics was held in a briefing room with the senior members of the Bahrain detachment. The consensus was that since we considered ourselves to now have air superiority, there was no need to risk further operations at low-level through AAA barrages, particularly if the Americans would agree to provide air support for us.'

For Sqn Ldr Risdale, too, 'this third mission was an emotional watershed. After returning to my room, I mulled over what we'd been through and had a bit of a cry. As a team, we were all quite private about such emotional hiccups, but I don't think any of us were immune.'

Later that day, Bahrain's second eight-ship launched to attack the airfield at An Najaf from medium-level. A single aiming point was chosen in the middle of the parallel runways, the idea being that ballistic dispersion would scatter the bombs and blanket the entire airfield area. The formation, led by Sqn Ldrs Mason and Stapleton, rendezvoused with two Victor tankers, which led them along the 'Olive Trail' – a 200-mile tanker-trail route towards the Saudi/Iraqi border.

The ingress route to An Najaf took about 40 minutes, and a strong upper wind caused some problems because the Tornados were forced to fly at an uncomfortably low airspeed in order to keep to their pre-planned timings. A further snag was that both the lead and No 3 aircraft reported that their GMRs had failed. This meant that they would have to fly in close formation on their wingmen (at night) and release their weapons when they saw the wingmen drop theirs. However, despite these setbacks, all eight aircraft arrived over the target on time.

Until then, the formation had been unopposed, but Flt Lt Paisey described how 'the defences opened up only after the first bombs impacted. The AAA was heavy and consisted of both tracer and airburst, reaching a height of approximately 18,000 ft. No SAMs were launched and there were no RHWR indications. Eight Tornados had dropped 64 1000-lb bombs on the target in one minute.'

Armed with eight 1000-lb freefall bombs, Tornado GR 1 ZA374/CN from the Dhahran Wing climbs through the clouds on its way to attack a target in Iraq (*Andy Glover*)

For the egress from the target, the effects of the winds were reversed and this time the crews had to use reheat to accelerate to a fast-enough speed to keep to the planned timings.

At Dhahran, Sqn Ldrs D Moule and C Coulls had spent a frustrating evening planning to use cluster bomb units for an attack on a Scud battery, which had been located by a reconnaissance aircraft. Unfortunately, by the time all the work to co-ordinate the mission was completed it was daylight, and the sortie was cancelled. Instead, the crews were re-tasked for the following night.

'The target was another major Iraqi airfield, Jalibah, which looked like a relatively unpleasant place to go to', recalled Coulls. 'As the mission was to "harass" operations from the airfield, we opted for the first four aircraft lofting 1000-lb airburst-fused bombs along the line of the AAA defences, closely followed by the second four attacking the runways and taxiways with JP233 from an entirely different direction. We were packaged with other units attacking targets in the general vicinity, and would, therefore, benefit from their support.' In fact, the second four-ship was later re-roled to carry 1000-lb bombs as well. The Dhahran Wing had taken a slightly different tactical solution to that at Bahrain by opting to loft five, rather than eight, 1000-lb bombs. This gave the aircraft a little more performance margin during the run-in for the attack and the loft manoeuvre itself.

The mission did not start well. One of the pilots cut his head badly while walking out to his aeroplane and could not fly the sortie. Then, when Sqn Ldrs Moule and Coulls got airborne, they suffered a number of systems failures in their aircraft. However, they decided to press on. 'The rendezvous with our tanker was successful', Coulls continued, 'and we were finally on our way.

'At this point, it is worth mentioning that the weather during the first week of *Desert Storm* was very poor. Our transit altitude was at about 10,000-12,000 ft, which tonight was exactly coincident with the cloud tops. This put us in and out of cloud when on the tanker, and meant we suffered moderate-to-severe turbulence for most of the transit. It was very uncomfortable, and a real testament to the skill of the pilots to get safely into contact with the refuelling basket. However, we eventually got to the drop-off point, still in bad weather, and turned north towards the Iraqi border, lights out and in radio silence. We started our descent and actually broke out into some clear air for a while. We were still concerned about the accuracy of our nav system, and tried to spot one of the other formation members, not surprisingly without success.

'At this point we decided that the best thing to do was to get to low-level earlier than planned, thus keeping us clear of the rest of the formation. We were also running a little early on our timeline, and consequently were flying much slower than our planned cruise speed, but were still in friendly territory. As we approached the border, we accelerated and dropped down to 200 ft using the automatic TFR, straight into dense fog – probably the last thing we were expecting to find in the desert.

'Then, as we accelerated through exactly 400 knots, the aircraft entered what was known as an open-loop pull up, which is pretty much like it sounds, climbing the aircraft steeply away from the ground. This necessitated cancelling the automatics and manually settling the aircraft back down to low-level. Unfortunately, the automatics refused to remain engaged above 400 knots, and Douglas had to fly the aircraft manually, very close to the ground, in cloud, with both of us using the radars to monitor our ground clearance. This was something that we had practised in the simulator (Cold War mentality!), and should really have stayed there. We pressed on like this for far too long until we finally saw sense. We were a hazard to ourselves and the rest of our team, so, thoroughly disappointed, we turned and headed back south just before we had planned to converge on the target.' The remaining aircraft prosecuted their attack successfully, although two of them sustained battle damage.

That evening, another eight-ship formation took off from Tabuk, bound for Al Taqaddum airfield, and it too seemed to be plagued by bad luck. 'We had a full bomb and fuel load, got airborne, then hit a snag', recalled Sqn Ldr Batson, in the lead aircraft. 'The control column would not move much to the right. I handed over the lead of the sortie and then went to a pre-designated area to jettison the bombs and dump some fuel, the idea being that if we lightened the aircraft we might be able to invert it – if there was something just jamming the controls, we would shake it out. We shook the aircraft around for about half-an-hour but couldn't fix the problem, so we flew back to base to attempt a landing.

'Every time I lined the aircraft up with the runway, the wind blew us off. I'd been trying to land for about an hour, making several approaches to a variety of runways at Tabuk, but all to no avail. The senior RAF supervisor at Tabuk then ordered us to abandon the aircraft. The transit to the abandonment area was occupied with running through the drills in the FRCs [Flight Reference Cards], with both of us preparing for an ejection from about 6000 ft above the ground. The Saudis launched a rescue helicopter when they knew we were just about to eject, presumably to avoid it being hit by anything raining down from on high. I discussed with Mike who would do the countdown, but as he was going to initiate command ejection for us both, it was decided that he would do the count – we agreed a countdown of ten.

'I remember the ejection as if I were watching a slow-motion film. It seemed like a lifetime before anything happened, although in fact it only took 0.6 of a second between Mike pulling the handle and the cockpit canopy flying off. There was an enormous bang, and I was hit in the right eye by something as my head was forced into my lap. Then I remember that although it was pitch black, there was this vast pool of white light from the flash of the ejection rocket's explosion. As we were taught, I started checking from top to bottom to ensure the parachute had deployed, and then located and released my dinghy pack once I saw the ground approaching.

'I had seen Mike some distance off during the descent, but he was above me. Rightly, as he went first, he should have been below me. I checked the parachute again and found it had a rip in one gore, allowing me to descend a spot quicker than normal. It was quite a pleasant descent really. I was able to see the circular irrigation fields and several small lights dotted around the area. As the ground appeared closer, I got into the parachute landing position and waited for the inevitable. After several seconds it did not come, so I relaxed, as I presumed I had estimated the closure incorrectly. Then I hit the ground and landed like a bag of spuds – no front left or right parachute landing for me.'

Meanwhile, something of a shambles ensued with rest of the formation. 'The No 2 took over and then AWACS delayed the mission by 20 minutes', declared Flt Lt Hawkins in the No 5 aircraft. 'There was indecision, and it ended up with me calling over the radio "who wants to come with me?" We proceeded as a five-ship and completed the task against Al Taqaddum.'

Eight aircraft from Tabuk led by Sqn Ldrs McAlpine and Pittaway carried out a low-level attack against the airfield facilities at H3 airfield in the early hours of 21 January. Once again, the aircraft carried eight 1000-lb bombs, which they delivered successfully from a loft profile. However, the Tornado missions flown that evening reflected a move towards operating at medium-level.

Tornado GR 1 ZD790/D from the Bahrain Wing was returning to base following another mission when this photograph was taken. By the beginning of February, the aircraft were beginning to look very tatty as the 'Desert Pink' paint had been badly eroded and faded by months of high-tempo flying in harsh desert conditions (*Stu Osborne*)

CHAPTER FOUR

MEDIUM-LEVEL OPERATIONS

By now it was clear that future Tornado GR 1 operations would be carried out at medium-level. In Sqn Ldr Coulls' view, 'to say that this was something of a culture shock to us is an understatement. Medium-level tactics had not been widely practised by the Tornado force, and the majority of the crews had no experience of them whatsoever. The facts were that the RAF had lost a number of aircraft during the opening week and we knew that the low-level tactics had been at least a contributory factor in all cases, whether the cause of the loss had been due to enemy action, or controlled flight into the ground. Flying above 20,000 ft would obviously negate the risk of hitting the ground, and also take us above the reach of AAA and tactical SAMs, or so the intelligence told us.'

'When I flew in the first medium-level mission of the war, I was very uneasy', agreed Sqn Ldr Buckley. 'All of our training during the Cold War and up to now had been at low-level, and night medium-level tactics are quite different. It all hinges on keeping a safe distance from the rest of the formation around you. At the altitudes we were flying, the all-up weight of the aircraft meant that speed control was critical and keeping formation position was quite difficult to achieve.'

For the 21 January evening sortie from Bahrain, eight aircraft, each armed with eight 1000-lb bombs, were tasked against the airfield facilities at Jalibah. The mission was flown at medium-level and was supported by four F-4G *Wild Weasels* and a fighter escort of two F-15Cs. After refuelling,

Tornado GR 1 ZD707/BK, loaded with LGBs, from the Dhahran Wing closes on the starboard wing hose of a VC10K tanker during pre-strike refuelling. Precision-guided weapons proved so accurate that the standard weapon load was reduced from three bombs to two (*Andy Glover*)

the Tornados left the two VC10K tankers for the 30-minute flight to Jalibah. Once again, they encountered the strong upper winds, which forced them to fly uncomfortably slowly on the way into the target. On the route in, the Tornados were unchallenged, but the AAA barrage started as soon as the first weapons impacted. A number of SAMs were also launched ballistically, with no indications of guidance.

All the aircraft dropped their weapons inside a two-minute window and started to head to the safety of the Saudi border, but the effects of the wind meant that they had to use reheat to keep to their time plan. The egress was made all the more exciting by radar lock-ups, which the RHWR identified as MiG-29 'Fulcrum' and Mirage F1EQ fighters – the two types in the IrAF inventory with a night capability. Later analysis showed that these were, in reality, other friendly fighters, but in the heat of the moment most of the formation had jettisoned their fuel tanks and twin-store carriers in attempts to break the lock. Two Victor tankers were on hand as the formation crossed back into Saudi airspace. However, the drama was far from over. As the Tornados approached Bahrain they found themselves in the midst of a Scud missile alert.

Two hours later, Sqn Ldr Whittingham and Flt Lt Baldwin led the first medium-level mission from Dhahran. Following a similar profile to the Bahrain-based Tornados, the six aircraft also attacked the airfield at Jalibah, each dropping five 1000-lb bombs on the HAS sites. Flt Lt Grout, the navigator in the No 3 aircraft, described the sortie as follows;

'Planning and briefing complete, the crew-in went well, we were all serviceable and we took-off in good order. The tankers were exactly where we expected them, and the AAR went according to plan, with all aircraft plugging in and getting the correct fuel. All was well in our little dark world. We checked in with AWACS, turned off the lights and crossed the border. As we approached the built-up areas, initially, we were over desert.

Most missions by Tornado GR 1s were supported by Victor or VC10K tankers for pre-strike refuelling. Here, LGB-armed Tornado GR 1 ZA399/G 'Granny' from the Bahrain Wing holds station off the Victor's port wing. The tanker is from No 55 Sqn (*Stu Osborne*)

The sky ahead soon lit up with a myriad of swirling AAA fire, mainly tracer. It looked like a deadly 4th of July party. I remember the odd expletive issuing from my mouth, as we steadily got closer. We had to go through this fire, as there was no alternative direction to attack from.

'I was now half heads-in looking for offsets and half out watching the tracer display, whilst in between tightening my straps and making sure all my kit was stowed snuggly in my flying clothing. I'm sure there was some buttock clenching in the mix as well. The feeling was more apprehensive than frightening.

'As we progressed nearer to the target, it became clear that the AAA was of small calibre and was not reaching our altitude – phew, relief. However, there was no time to relax, as we still had to keep a good lookout for any missile launch as the Iraqis had by now started to fire SAMs without using radar.

'Bombs away, lots of bright flashes from the 40 bombs dropped by our eight jets, and now the run for home. As we crossed the "lights on" line, the sky became a mixture of stars and aircraft lights. Our accurate plan in-bound to the target had become a bit of a shambles out-bound, and we were not sure which aircraft were ours. This, added to the fact that there were numerous tankers waiting for several different missions, made the initial part of the recovery somewhat haphazard. Some bright spark transmitted for his formation to drop a flare – he got more responses than he bargained for. Eventually, we all got our acts together, refuelled and came home. Four hours and 25 minutes passed in a flash. There was a great sense of relief that the mission had been successful, and that we had all survived another day.'

In the No 4 aircraft, Flt Lts P Reid and S Hadley were experiencing the Iraqi air defences for the first time. 'I took Fix/Attack mode at 40 nautical miles to make sure that I nailed the target', recalled Flt Lt Hadley. 'A minute or so later, we saw our first AAA – a massive red bursting carpet of small explosions at around 10,000-15,000 ft, perfectly visible against the total blackness of the empty desert. Then some more, this time white streaks snaking up from some sort of rapid-fire AAA, much lower in altitude. It wasn't scary, but at the same time it was rather mesmerising. Just as we were about to drop as part of the lead four-ship, the bombs from the Nos 1 and 2 aircraft impacted, with a series of brilliant white flashes in rapid succession marking where the sticks of bombs hit. They really lit up the night.'

Meanwhile, at Tabuk, Flt Lts Roche and Bellamy had been tasked to lead an ALARM formation to provide SEAD support for an operation by F-15Es. 'On the night of 21 January, four ALARM-equipped Tornados performed a graceful fan-split at low-level to spread-launch 12 missiles at radars located around Al-Qaim, close to the Syrian border', recounted Flt Lt Bellamy. 'This mission was in support of 14 F-15E Strike Eagles, who released weapons from an altitude of 30,000 ft. On return to Tabuk, the ALARM crews were greeted with groundcrew in full NBC attire and the

As operations continued, unofficial nose art started to appear on Tornado GR 1s at all three bases. This elevated view is of the flightline at Tabuk, where the aircraft were decorated with shark's mouths. The jet in the foreground is ZA447/EA *MiG Eater* (*Tim Marsh*)

eventual realisation that the F-15Es had bombed a very suspicious target – an anthrax production facility.'

As the ALARM formation was recovering to Tabuk, one of the last low-level missions was about to get airborne, with a ToT in the early hours of 22 January. The eight aircraft led by Sqn Ldrs Lennox and Weeks, each armed with five 1000-lb bombs, were bound for the radar facility at Ar Rutbah. Unfortunately, this mission was not blessed with good luck. Firstly, three aircraft had to pull out before crossing the border because of systems failures, and then the lead Tornado was shot down over the target and both crew members were killed.

That afternoon, Flt Lts Fenlon-Smith and Hawkins led another eight aircraft from Tabuk at medium-level, supported by two ALARM Tornados, against an ammunition storage facility at Qubaysah, to the west of Ar Ramadi. However, the other Tornado missions over the next three days, all of which were carried out at medium-level and at night, continued the work of harassing and neutralising the IrAF's main operating bases. Sqn Ldr Risdale and Wg Cdr Broadbent led an eight-ship from Bahrain against Tallil, and Wg Cdr Witts and Flt Lt Smith led an eight-ship from Dhahran against Shaibah on 22 January.

'At this higher altitude things seemed much more pedestrian', thought Witts, 'and, of course, there was the added grandstand view of southern Iraq and Kuwait, where the darkness was periodically punctuated by fires and explosions. AAA was still trying its best to reach us but, now, we could look down almost contemptuously on the streams of tracer as they whirled about beneath us. There were a few pockets of large-calibre AAA that could reach our operating altitude, but we tried to stay well clear of those. On the other hand, SAMs were now much more of a threat, although the campaign to defeat them was having considerable success. USAF *Wild Weasels* would attack any missile radar that threatened, and the Iraqis were starting to fire their SAMs in an unguided mode, rather than turn on their radars and attract the *Weasels'* lethal attention. On this trip, we saw a few missiles arcing up nearby, but nothing that threatened us directly.'

The following day the Bahrain Wing (led by Sqn Ldrs Taylor and Thwaites) bombed Mudaysis airfield, and formations from Tabuk (led by Flt Lts M Williams and Goddard) and Dhahran (led by Sqn Ldrs Moule and Coulls) attacked Al Taqaddum. Sqn Ldr Coulls remembered that 'the target ingress and egress involved a lengthy transit over the heavily built-up areas to the south and west of the city of Baghdad, and whilst the air defence network was no longer integrated, individual SAMs were capable of autonomous operation.

'As we proceeded north, with about 60 miles to run to the outskirts of Baghdad, all hell broke loose below us. We had some collective experience of ground fires at this point, but had seen nothing like this. We could make out AAA, with numerous colours of tracer and trajectory. There were missiles, presumably unguided and again with different coloured trails, fortunately all topping out below us – it looked like the intelligence might be right after all. Some of the fires looked like they might only be flares, fired for effect, but we had no real way of knowing. This intense display continued for at least the next 15 minutes until we were well clear of the target, and is a sight that we will never forget.

'We were also happy that our bombs had impacted close to the aim point – there was enough ambient light to see the ground and make out the features on the airfield, and we managed to arrange our off-target manoeuvre in order to see the bombs' strike. To help, there was some low-lying mist on the airfield, and we could see the shockwaves travelling outwards from the impact points. As we manoeuvred off target, we were locked-up by a SAM-3 target tracking radar, which we knew was there, but our countermeasures procedures seemed to work and the lock was broken.'

On 24 January the Tabuk Wing bombed the barracks at H3 airfield. The mission was successful, but Flt Lt Hawkins recalled that 'there was very heavy large-calibre AAA coming up to 20,000 ft plus. I found myself trying to stand up to get my backside away, so I told myself "sit down, you silly fool" – as if another three inches would have helped.' In the No 5 aircraft. Flt Lt Klein also noted 'heavy AAA up to 21,000 ft', and Flt Lt T J Marsh, on his first operational mission, with Flt Lt K A Smith, remembered 'lots of fireworks that night, very colourful with red and orange tracer – apparently Soviet-supplied or home produced was what made the difference in colour'.

The mission flown from Dhahran that evening against Al Rumaylah was less successful and resulted in the loss of one Tornado and the near loss of another. The first four of the eight aircraft had been loaded with 'proximity'-fused bombs, with the intention that the weapons would explode above the ground to keep down the heads of the AAA gunners so that the rear four could concentrate on the HAS areas with impact-fused bombs. Perhaps luckily for them, two of the first four aborted their sorties after technical difficulties and had to return to Dhahran. The remaining two pressed on to Al Rumaylah and were severely damaged over the target. Flt Lts S J Burgess and R Ankerson were forced to abandon their aircraft immediately and they became prisoners of war. Meanwhile, Flt Lts S Gillies and S P Rochelle coaxed their badly damaged Tornado back to Dhahran. It was only when the aircraft was inspected after landing at the base that the awful truth became apparent – the proximity-fuses had detonated right under the aircraft and both Tornados had been damaged by their own weapons.

By 25 January the IrAF had been effectively neutralised, and the targeting for the Tornado GR 1 force switched to Iraqi communications systems, power distribution centres and ammunition storage dumps. On that day Flt Lts Fenlon-Smith and Hawkins led an eight-ship from Tabuk against the petroleum storage facility at H3, and on the 26th the same crew led another eight aircraft, at low-level this time, against the tropospheric scatter aerials at Ad Diwaniyah and Al Kufah. Both of these missions were supported by ALARM-carrying

Sgt Phil Reed inspects damage caused to Tornado GR 1 ZD843/DH of the Dhahran Wing when its proximity-fused bombs exploded under the aircraft on 24 January. The crew, Flt Lts Stu Gillies and Pete Rochelle, had a lucky escape (*Les Hendry*)

Tornados, although by now stocks of the weapon were depleted, so the SEAD aircraft carried only two missiles each.

Of the low-level loft sortie against Al Kufah, the newly-arrived Flt Lt T J Marsh commented that 'this attack was planned for accuracy at low-level as a loft delivery, due to the analysis of the likely defences. It was not an unexpected change of tactics, just a rational decision by the lead crews. The attack was extremely distracting for me, being at the back of the package and experiencing the reflections and flashes in the HUD and on the canopy, plus all the AAA.'

Meanwhile, Flt Lt C C Drewery and Sqn Ldr H E Newton led eight Tornado GR 1s from Dhahran against the power station at An Nasiriyah and, after their leader aborted, Flt Lts Scott and M A Jeffery found themselves at the front of five aircraft bombing the ammunition depot at Khran Al Mahawil.

The previous day, the Bahrain Wing had been tasked with bombing the Al Zubayr oil pumping station, close to the Iranian border. In a departure from the practice until then, it was decided that this mission would not carry out AAR on the out-bound leg and instead would rendezvous with the tankers on the return leg. This change meant that without full fuel tanks the Tornado GR 1s would be much lighter and could, therefore, climb higher for the ingress to the target area. The routing to the target was along the coast, and Flt Lt Paisey in the No 4 aircraft wrote that 'very little AAA was encountered on coasting into Iraq, but the Tigris-Euphrates Delta lit up with pinpoints of light denoting light AAA. However, it was not until weapons started falling on the target that heavy AAA opened up, with snaking lines of tracer weaving through the sky beneath the formation. Some shells exploded at around 18,000 ft. Several crews saw unguided missile launches, which arced above the aircraft.' The target stood out well on radar, and all crews were confident of good hits. The next day (26 January) Sqn Ldr Risdale and Wg Cdr Broadbent led the wing against the ammunition depot at Tall Al Lahm, near Jalibah.

A second mission by the Bahrain Wing on the 26th brought home the challenges of AAR in difficult conditions. It was planned as a ten-ship formation against an electronics facility at An Nasiriyah, but in the event thick cloud and strong turbulence meant that only four aircraft were able to refuel successfully. Of these four, one had to turn back shortly after crossing the border because of a systems failure.

After attacks the previous day by eight aircraft from Tabuk on the communications facility at Ar Rutbah and by an identical number of jets from Dhahran on the ammunition depot at Rumaylah, a concerted effort started on 28 January to target Iraqi fuel storage depots. The dump at H3 was attacked by ten aircraft from Tabuk in the morning and a further 12 aircraft from Tabuk hit the depot at Haditha that evening. Eight aircraft from Dhahran attacked the dump at Uwayjah and ten from Bahrain hit An Najaf. After impressive explosions gave evidence of direct hits, Sqn Ldr Risdale, who led an eight-ship from Bahrain to the oil refinery at As Samawah, commented that 'there was no need for the BDA pictures'. The following day, an eight-ship from Dhahran bombed the Sayyadah petroleum facility, Al Taqaddum airfield was revisited by ten more Tornado GR 1s from Tabuk and eight aircraft from Bahrain attacked the petroleum facility at Ad Diwaniyah.

The pattern continued over the next four days. During that period, the Tornado GR 1 force from all three bases attacked airfield facilities at Al Jarrah, Taqaddum and Q'alat Salih, the SAM supply facility at Shaibah, the EW site at Wadi Al Khirr and petroleum storage and pumping stations at Ar Ramadi, Al Hillah and H2. The Bahrain Wing also attacked the Republican Guard barracks in Kuwait on 30 January. However, while these attacks caused a degree of 'harassment', the Tornado GR 1 weapon aiming system was not precise enough from medium-level to ensure that small targets, such as individual buildings within a complex, were hit accurately enough to do lasting damage. Radar-aimed bombing at night had reached its limitations, and a new tactic was clearly needed.

LASER GUIDANCE 1 – PAVE SPIKE

From its earliest days at Laarbruch, the Tornado GR 1 had demonstrated the ability to drop Laser-Guided Bombs (LGBs) in co-operative attacks with AN/AVQ-23E Pave Spike laser targeting pod-equipped Buccaneers. It was now hoped that this low-level technique could be adapted for medium-level operations in the Gulf. Six Buccaneers of No 208 Sqn duly deployed from Lossiemouth, Scotland, to Bahrain in the last week of January, and on the 30th and 31st a number of training sorties were flown over Saudi Arabia with Tornados from both Bahrain and Tabuk to iron out the tactics.

Referring to the Cold War Option Lima, Sqn Ldr Coulls found that 'interestingly, when we eventually got into the LGB business with the Buccs in Iraq in 1991, the tactics that we had developed for low-level ops in Germany formed the basis for what we used at medium-level there. And many of the characters were the same on both forces!'

The first LGB mission was flown on 3 February, with Sqn Ldrs Mason and Stapleton leading a mixed formation of four Tornado GR 1s and three Buccaneers against the highway bridge at As Samawah – one of three bridges across the river Euphrates within the city. Each Tornado was armed with three LGBs, and the intention was to operate as sub-formations of two Tornado GR 1 bombers and one Buccaneer designator attacking two minutes apart. The third Buccaneer acted as an airborne spare, but was not needed.

After AAR from two VC10K tankers, the formations crossed into Iraqi airspace. Initially the crews found themselves in thick cloud, which forced each three-ship into close formation. The discomfort of being in close formation in enemy airspace was exacerbated by the disparity of speeds

A typical tactical formation in the second month of the Gulf War – Tornado GR 1 ZD895/BF of the Dhahran Wing is accompanied by a Bahrain-based Pave Spike-equipped Buccaneer S2B of No 208 Sqn (*Andy Glover*)

LGB-armed Tornado GR 1s ZD715/DB and ZA461/DK from the Dhahran Wing refuel from a Victor tanker of No 55 Sqn, while the crew of a Pave Spike Buccaneer patiently waits for the AAR evolution to be completed. All three aircraft would then head into Iraq (*Andy Glover*)

between the two different types, but the skies soon cleared, giving ideal clear weather for laser operations. Unfortunately, three of the bombs dropped by the first pair did not guide because the wrong laser codes had been set. However, all of the remaining attacks were successful.

Later that day Flt Lt Thomson and Sqn Ldr Sinclair led another four Bahrain Wing Tornado GR 1s, supported by three Buccaneers, for an LGB attack on the Muftal Wadam bridge over the Euphrates at As Samawah. This attack was entirely successful, as was another one carried out by the same crews the following day against one of the bridges at An Nasiriyah. Sqn Ldrs Mason and Stapleton also led their second LGB attack on 4 February, this time against the road bridge over the Euphrates at Al Madinah, just to the west of Qurna. Although one of the four Tornado GR 1s and one of the Buccaneers became unserviceable, the remaining aircraft pressed home successful attacks, the first two aircraft dropping the southern span of the bridge and the last one dropping the northern span. 'During the bombing run traffic was seen on the bridge', noted Flt Lt Paisey. 'At the first impact, the traffic stopped and was seen to reverse, only to see the other end of the bridge explode. He remained on the intact centre span, no doubt surprised and relieved.'

Meanwhile, on the night of 3 February, the Bahrain Wing launched an eight-ship night wave led by Sqn Ldrs Taylor and Thwaites against the ammunition storage facility at Tall Al Lahm, using freefall bombs.

Sqn Ldr Risdale and Wg Cdr Broadbent led their four-ship against the remaining suspension bridge over the river Euphrates at As Samawah on 5 February, and also visited An Nasiriyah the following day. Sqn Ldrs Moule and Coulls led the first LGB sortie from Dhahran on 5 February. The target for the four Tornado GR 1s was a large road bridge over the river Tigris at Al Kut.

'The rendezvous, tanking and target ingress went like clockwork', recalled Coulls, 'and we settled on the target run. All was going well until shortly before weapons release, when there was a radio call from our designator asking which bridge we were aiming at – with only seconds to go until weapons release, confusion reigned! However, we were cleared to drop just in time, and as we manoeuvred off target, it was suddenly apparent what the problem had been. The target bridge had already been hit and one end of it was lying in the river. The Buccaneer navigator had been able to see all of this with his targeting pod. There was another large bridge in the city about a kilometre from ours. In the event, our bombs were guided into the bridge's buttresses at one end, completing the job that somebody else had started.'

Since Pave Spike was a purely optical system, it was limited to daylight only, so the LGB missions were all flown in daytime. In fact, the Tornado GR 1 force had already begun to shift towards daytime operations by 3 February. This was mainly to try to improve the accuracy of the bombing by delivering the weapons visually from a high-angle dive where possible. The new tactics were also used for the first time on 3 February when day waves were launched, carrying freefall bombs, from the Dhahran and Tabuk Wings respectively against storage warehouses at As Samawah and ammunition storage at Qubaysah, and from Bahrain against the ammunition storage facility at Tall Al Lahm. On 4 February the Tabuk Wing launched three four-ships to attack the ammunition depot at Karbala, and the following day the wing targeted the power station at Al Musayib and, later, the petroleum production plant at Al Hillah. Meanwhile, the Dhahran Wing took on airfield facilities at Al Jarrah and joined the Bahrain Wing in a mission against the petroleum storage depot at An Nasiriyah.

Flt Lt Mike Warren and Flg Off Mal Craghill from the Tabuk Wing smile for the camera from the cockpit of Tornado GR 1 ZA465/FK *FOXY KILLER* prior to taking part in a six-ship attack on the Ar Ramadi highway bridge on 18 February (*Kev Noble*)

Although the weapon accuracy was improved, the new tactics were not without their own problems. Flt Lt Klein, leading the attack on Al Musayib, reported missing the target because of high winds and unfamiliarity with the high-angle dive manoeuvre. Unfortunately, too, the weather was not always suitable for this delivery profile because of cloud obscuring the target area. Night attacks continued, as well, with targets including Shaykh Mazhar ammunition depot (Dhahran Wing), Al Iskandariyah ammunition plant (Tabuk Wing) and As Samawah petroleum storage (Dhahran Wing).

On 6 February there were daylight raids by the Tabuk Wing against the airfield facilities at H3 Southwest and by the Dhahran Wing against the Al Jarrah SAM support facility – the Bahrain Wing also attacked Al Jarrah that day, concentrating on the hangar buildings. That evening, eight Tornado GR 1s, with support from a pair of ALARM aircraft, took off from Tabuk to revisit the power station at Al Musayib.

'The refuelling and transit were uneventful as we crossed into Iraq and headed for Baghdad on another clear night', recalled Flt Lt Craghill in the No 4 aircraft. 'This would turn out to be to our advantage. As we entered what had become known as the "super-MEZ" (the Missile Engagement Zone of the many SAM sites around Baghdad), it became clear that our presence would not go unchallenged. Despite the pre-planned firings of a number of ALARMs, the Iraqi defences were very active. Part of our pre-war training had been a focus on not just the capabilities of Iraq's many SAMs, but their key visual characteristics at launch. Knowing the colour of the missile's rocket flame, and typical salvo sizes of missiles fired, meant we would be able to identify what was being launched. On this particular night we watched in amazement as, far below us, salvos of SAM-8, SAM-3 and SAM-6 missiles were fired off, seemingly without guidance due to the threat of anti-radiation missile attack. The Iraqis wanted to be seen to be doing something, but didn't want to get themselves killed in the process.

'Not all operators were so timid. As we ran in towards the target, with armament safety switches live, bombs primed and the target identified on radar, Mike and I received indications on the RHWR of SAM-2 target acquisition radar. This had become relatively common, but as we monitored the display the audio alarm sounded to warn of a SAM-2 target tracking radar. I dispensed chaff and confirmed to Mike that the jamming pod was responding correctly. We now had only a few miles to run to weapons release – perhaps ten seconds – when the unthinkable happened. The alarm switched to a ferocious warble, the display changed to SAM-2 missile guidance, and as we looked out in the direction of the "spike" we saw an almighty flash as a single massive missile came off the launcher. There could be no doubt that a SAM-2 was coming straight for us.

'We quickly agreed to complete the attack, now only seconds away, and then defend against the missile. I made a call on the strike primary frequency that we were defending against a SAM-2, with our location, to cue our electronic attack support. One thing on our side was that the missile had been fired at fairly short range, so we were able to track its position from the burning rocket plume throughout most of its flight. I kept dispensing chaff, and as soon as we felt our bombs' release Mike hauled the aircraft into a descending right-hand turn towards the missile as I called out heights and speed. Our aim was to turn tight inside the missile's flight path, making it pull hard to keep track of us and hopefully increasing its miss distance. Somewhere close behind us there was a bright flash as the missile detonated, whether on proximity to us or based on a pre-programmed altitude we didn't know, and somehow we had escaped unscathed.

'Mike put the aircraft into a climb in full afterburner – uncomfortably highlighting our position in the darkness, but essential to regain height and energy in case of another attack – and we rejoined the formation for the egress southwest across Iraq. Luckily for us there was an emergency refuelling track just south of the border where we were able to replace the fuel lost in defending against the SAM-2, and we made an uneventful recovery to base. Back on the ground, debriefing with our colleagues, it hit home just how close we had come to being hit by that missile when several of the aircraft ahead of us on the attack claimed that it had gone off "just behind" them. What saved us was our training, and the fact that we knew each other so well by this point, each trusting the other to do whatever was required. That, and a huge dose of luck.'

Tornado GR 1 operations on the next two days consisted entirely of daylight raids against oil or petroleum facilities by

This was the view from the cockpit of Tornado GR 1 ZA446/EF as the Tabuk Wing crew of Flt Lts Tim Marsh and Ken Smith recovered from a dive attack on the oil refinery at Haditha on 7 February. Their stick of five bombs can be seen exploding just above the wingtip, with black smoke coming from the centre bomb strike (*Tim Marsh*)

aircraft dropping freefall bombs or attacks on bridges by aircraft dropping LGBs. When the Tabuk Wing sent eight aircraft to Haditha, Flt Lt Hawkins commented 'we went against Haditha petrol facility using a steep dive/toss profile. We were leading, and achieved a direct hit with five 1000-lb bombs, which set it alight. Pete called "it's a burner" over the radio. Very satisfying!'

Although the ground-attack wings had shifted from low-level to medium-level and from night to daytime, the reconnaissance detachment at Dhahran continued to operate under the cover of darkness at low-level. Typically, two or three Tornado GR 1As would launch each night, and the sorties were planned to be flown at between 550-600 knots. The usual tasking included line searches along 'standard routes' in the desert to the west of Kuwait on the way to cover areas deeper in Iraq. It was not until the outbreak of the land war that crews realised those line searches had been intended to ensure that the area was clear of Iraqi forces.

Most of the early reconnaissance sorties were 'Scud Hunting' missions aimed at locating Iraqi Scud batteries, which were deployed somewhere in the vastness of the desert. A number of Scud batteries were successfully found, but the images brought back by reconnaissance aircraft also included other systems and equipment such as P-14 'Tall King' early warning radar, T-55 tanks, SA-8 batteries and towed artillery.

Some of the reconnaissance crews experienced exciting moments, like Flt Lts B Robinson and H G Walker who suffered a generator failure and temporary loss of the entire electrical system to the southwest of Tallil on 31 January. Having lost all of their EW self-protection and most of their navigation systems, the crew managed to zoom climb and dash for the sanctuary of Saudi airspace. Two nights later the same crew had more excitement when their aircraft was in collision with the Tornado GR 1A of Wg Cdr Torpy and Flt Lt T Perrem. Fortunately, no lasting damage was done to either aircraft.

LASER GUIDANCE 2 – TIALD

During the 1980s Ferranti Ltd had been involved in a project to provide the RAF with a 'home-grown' laser designating capability. The result of the company's research was the Thermal Imaging Airborne Laser Designator (TIALD) pod, and the project was at a research and development stage in late 1990. With deployment to the Gulf looming later in the year, the RAF asked Ferranti to accelerate development of the pod so that it could be used operationally if needed over Iraq. This they managed to do, and on 24 January 1991 four crews from No 13 Sqn deployed to Boscombe Down, Wiltshire, to take part in Trial *Albert* to prove the TIALD pod for operational service.

Flt Lts Kev Ward and Jerry Cass did much of the development trials work for the TIALD pod, and then went on to prove the system's worth during operational sorties from Tabuk (*Kev Noble*)

A VC10K tanker refuels LGB-armed Tornado GR 1 ZD845/AF *Angel Face* from the Tabuk Wing. The aircraft beyond it is the TIALD-equipped designator for the Tornado flight (*Lars Smith*)

Among the crews involved were Flt Lts K G Noble and J M Cass, who had just graduated from the Qualified Weapons Instructor course. They duly designated the first successful LGB drop at Garvie Island, off the northwest coast of Scotland, on 2 February. Four days later, the No 13 Sqn crews left Honington behind a TriStar tanker for the long trail to Tabuk. At this stage only two prototype TIALD pods existed and they, too, were despatched to Tabuk.

Once in-theatre, the TIALD project was taken over by Wg Cdr R Iveson and his navigator Flt Lt C C Purkiss. After a trial drop on the nearby Badr range on the night of 8 February, TIALD was cleared for operations and Iveson and Purkiss flew the first sortie on 10 February. The targets were the HASs on H3 Southwest airfield, and the tactics mirrored those already being used successfully by the Bahrain and Dhahran Wings, with one designator working with two bombers.

With the stock of ALARM almost used up and the Iraqi air defence system virtually shut down, the ALARM-qualified crews found themselves back in the conventional bombing role. Flt Lts Noble and Cass flew their first operational TIALD sortie on the night of 11 February, targeting the HASs on H3 Northwest airfield. By now it was clear that just two LGBs were enough to destroy a HAS, so weapons loads were reduced accordingly. The advantage of TIALD over Pave Spike was that its infra-red sensor enabled it to be used at night. More pilots and navigators were hastily trained to use the equipment to provide ten TIALD-qualified crews, which would allow almost round-the-clock operations. Thus, the two TIALD pods, by now nicknamed 'Tracy' and 'Sandra' after the 'Fat Slags' characters in the satirical magazine *Viz*, were used almost continuously.

From 9 to 11 February, while the Pave Spike/LGB formations had continued the work of destroying the bridges over the Euphrates and Tigris rivers, all three bases had also been launching four- or eight-ships armed with freefall bombs against ammunition depots and petroleum storage facilities. The ammunition stores at Al Iskandariyah, Tall Al Lahm, Habbaniyah and H3 were all attacked, and Sqn Ldrs Buckley and Teakle led eight aircraft from Bahrain to the petroleum storage plant at Uwayjah on 9 February. Sqn Ldr Whittingham and Flt Lt Baldwin led eight aircraft from Dhahran to the storage tanks at Basra the following day. During this mission, Flt Lts Turnbull and Grout dropped the 1000th 1000-lb bomb of the campaign. However, the fact that all of these targets had been attacked previously is perhaps an indication of the overall inaccuracy and ineffectiveness of dropping freefall bombs from medium-level.

On 12 February eight Tornado GR 1s from Bahrain led by Sqn Ldrs Taylor and Thwaites, plus a further eight from Dhahran led by Sqn Ldr W Hartree and Flt Lt R J Wesley, bombed the liquid propellant production plant at Latifiya, and Flt Lts Fenlon-Smith and Hawkins led seven aircraft from Tabuk to attack the EW site at Ar Ruwayshid. These were the last missions in which freefall weapons were used, and for the rest of the conflict Tornado GR 1s operated in pairs or four-ships dropping LGBs in co-operation with Pave Spike or TIALD designators.

A pair of LGB-armed Tornado GR 1s (the nearest aircraft is ZD847/CH) from the Dhahran Wing sets off for a mission over Iraq (*Andy Glover*)

Although laser guidance solved many of the weapon aiming problems from medium-level, it was no panacea. LGBs still had to be dropped accurately into the 'laser basket' – the relatively small area of sky in which the laser energy was reflected back. The correct laser codes had to be programmed into the weapons and the bombs had to be dropped within the tight timing schedule within which the designator marked each individual target. Even assuming that the weapon was dropped into the laser basket at the right time with the right codes set, there was always a chance that it still might not guide. There was also the chance that smoke or cloud might interrupt the laser lock and seduce the bomb away from the target. This might in any case occur if two targets were close to each other and the debris from one was blown into the laser field of view for the second. And, of course, the premise for all laser operations was that the weather was good enough for the designator to actually see the target.

Many of these points were driven home during an ambitious sortie from Bahrain on 12 February. Sqn Ldrs Mason and Stapleton led a four-ship of Tornado GR 1s and a pair of Buccaneers against HAS sites at both Al Taqaddum and Al Asad airfields. Each aircraft was loaded with three LGBs, and the intention was to drop two bombs on targets on the first airfield and the remaining one on targets at the second airfield. Each Pave Spike designator would mark two targets on each airfield. In the end, because of various mix-ups between designators and bombers, only one of the eight targets was hit. The problems, which included most of the 'gotchas' with laser-guided weapons, were largely caused because the crews had allocated too little time between individual attacks to allow the designators to find each specific target. But it was only through bold experiments such as this that the lessons could be learnt.

Over the next six days the Tornado GR 1s from all three wings were employed in systematically destroying every individual HAS on the IrAF main operating bases. The airfields at H2, H3, Al Amarah, Al Asad, Al Taqaddum, Al Jarrah, Tallil, Kut Al Hayy, Mudaysis, Jalibah, Q'alat Salih were all attacked over this period.

In comparison to the incredibly high-risk low-level operations, the medium-level LGB missions might, in the minds of some, have become something of a 'milk run'. The Iraqi defences seemed to have been reduced to sporadic AAA and the occasional launch of an unguided SAM. 'I think we must have got a bit complacent at that point', admitted Sqn Ldr Buckley, 'because we thought we could deal with these threats.' His own 'wake-up call' came on a mission to the west of Baghdad. 'This was a very hairy moment for Paddy and me', he later wrote. 'Not one SAM-3, but four were fired up at us. It was a perfectly clear day with no cloud, and I watched the trail of each missile as it raced upwards towards us. My intention was to roll the aircraft and pull towards the missile at some predetermined point that I couldn't specify if asked (I would have to apply a bit of "that looks about right"). However, happily for Paddy and me, the missiles all arched over well below the level of our aircraft and we were unscathed.'

Any complacency amongst the Tornado GR 1 force was certainly shattered on 14 February during a mission to destroy the HASs at Al Taqaddum. Led by Sqn Ldrs Mason and Stapleton, 12 aircraft from Bahrain, comprising eight Tornado GR 1s and four Buccaneers, were supported by four F-4G *Wild Weasels* and two EF-111 jammers. After joining two VC10K tankers to follow the 'Olive Trail', the formation pushed northwards into Iraq. All eight Tornado GR 1s followed the same attack track at 90-second intervals, and all scored direct hits on their target. However, as they turned off target, the Buccaneer designating for the last Tornado reported a double missile launch. Seventeen seconds later the Tornado, which was crewed by Flt Lts R J S G Clark and S M Hicks, was hit by a SAM and was seen to enter a shallow dive trailing smoke until it hit the ground to the east of the target area. Although no parachutes were seen by the rest of the formation, Flt Lt Clark was able to eject, but was captured. Flt Lt Hicks was killed. It was a sobering reminder that the Iraqi air defences should never be underestimated.

The next day, after leading his four-ship to destroy HASs at Tallil, Wg Cdr Witts commented that 'after the previous day's shoot down, we were a bit warier of the Iraqi defences, and with some cause at it turned out. We had attacked Tallil once again and, just after releasing our bombs, had been locked up by a SAM-6 which took a great deal of evasive effort to shake off.'

However, despite the loss of another Tornado GR 1, the campaign against the HAS sites was entirely successful. On 17 and 18 February there was a brief return to finish off the bridges over the river Euphrates at As Samawah, Ar Ramadi and Fallujah, but from 18 February the focus for operations moved to the operating surfaces and ancillary facilities on the airfields. Placed on critical points of the taxiways and runways, a single LGB could create a large enough crater to render the concrete unusable. Indeed, the weapon proved to be far more effective than the JP233. Furthermore, other small buildings that had been left unscathed by earlier attacks could now also be pinpointed.

Over Tallil once again on 18 February, Wg Cdr Witts reported that 'we were aiming at communications buildings, fuel storage areas and weapons storage. Despite some fairly active defensive AAA and SAM defences, we achieved some very satisfying explosions'. For Flt Lt Noble, 'the most memorable sortie was Al Jarrah on 19 February against the ammo dump – Jerry would normally just call "Splash" over the radio, which he did again this time, but immediately called "cor that went up" over the intercom. I dipped the wing to have a look and it was like a small atom bomb had gone off.'

Sqn Ldr Whittingham and Flt Lt Baldwin led another four-ship to Al Jarrah that afternoon. 'I was playing Billy Idol on the CVR [Cockpit Voice recorder] as we flew towards the target', recalled Flt Lt Hadley. 'I would turn it off before we got to the target area, where we had two SAM-2s straddling the target so that we had a 100 nautical mile SAM belt to thread our way through. Fortunately, the Ravens and *Wild Weasels* had been doing their job and the Iraqis were scared to turn on their radars.

'That day, the mayhem started slowly. First, the radar started to fail. After working it I got it up and running again, but then the HUD failed, and other bits of nav kit, and very quickly we got sucked into the drills to try to get the jet

Tornado GR 1 ZD792/CF *Nursie* from the Dhahran Wing breaks to starboard, revealing three Paveway LGBs beneath its fuselage (*Chris Coulls*)

working so that we could drop our bombs on target. Then we were into the SAM MEZs. Twice before target we were locked on by the SAM-2s, and twice we broke lock. Bombs dropped, the other SAM-2 lit us up twice, again causing us to go defensive to break lock. Eventually, after around 20 minutes of equipment failures, evading SAMs and bombing the target, everything went absolutely calm, almost in an instant.

'And as we powered away from the threats towards the tanker, I was suddenly aware of some music playing. It was Billy Idol. Still. I had tuned out the music the instant that the kit started failing and hadn't noticed it at all as we fought to break radar lock and press home the attack. Now that all was back to normal, and we were flying a high-level transit to the tanker and home, the music suddenly became audible again. I had just completed a highly intense war mission with rock music blaring in the background but I hadn't even noticed it. My brain just tuned it out to concentrate on the task at hand.'

Aircraft involved in most of the missions on 20 February against Shaibah, Q'alat Salih, Rumaylah and Kut Al Hayy brought their weapons back because poor weather obscured all of the targets. The cloudy weather continued into the next morning, but the skies had cleared enough on the afternoon of 21 February for successful sorties to be flown against Rumaylah by the Dhahran-based aircraft. However, missions against Shaibah (by the Tabuk Wing) and against Q'alat Salih and Kut Al Hayy (by the Bahrain Wing) were thwarted by the clouds. Two days of relatively good weather then followed, allowing the Tabuk Wing to neutralise Al Jarrah and Mudaysis, the Dhahran Wing to complete their work at Rumaylah and the Bahrain Wing to attack Kut Al Hayy and Q'alat Salih.

The ground war started on 23 February, and although it made little difference to the Tornado GR 1 force, the Tornado F 3s noticed an immediate change. 'From initially sitting some 80 miles south of the border', remarked Flt Lt Elliott, 'we now moved north of it. There were two main CAPs, As Salman in Iraq and overhead Kuwait City.'

From this day the skies began to fill with thick black smoke after Iraqi forces set light to the Kuwaiti oil wells. 'The sky was full of ominous black smoke up to about 9000 ft, all coming from Kuwait', wrote Wg Cdr Witts. 'We successfully attacked the airfield at Q'alat Salih north of Kuwait and not far from the Iraq-Iran border. It was a God-forsaken area, bearing indelible

A rare photograph records the instant that an LGB is dropped over Iraq by a Tornado GR 1 from the Tabuk Wing (*Tim Marsh*)

Tornado F 3 ZE199/W flies low over one of the oil wells in Kuwait that had been set ablaze by retreating Iraqi troops. This photograph was taken during one of the last Tornado F 3 CAPs, on 8 March 1991 (*Paul Lightbody*)

scars from Iraqi's previous long-standing conflict with Iran.' A formation from Bahrain led by Flt Lts Beet and Osborne was also tasked against Q'alat Salih that day. All three bases flew missions against Tallil, but only a handful of aircraft were able to drop their weapons. Sqn Ldr Risdale commented, tongue in cheek, 'the target was totally obscured by black smoke, so we took our bombs home, stacked for the day and went water skiing – hey ho!' The Tabuk and Dhahran Wings both attacked Jalibah on this day, but with mixed results.

The clouds returned over Iraq for the next two days, and daily missions mounted by Tornado GR 1s from both Dhahran and Bahrain against Al Taqaddum on 25 February were unsuccessful because of the weather conditions in the target area.

Further sorties against Shaykh Mazhar by Bahrain-based aircraft experienced similar difficulties the next day, as did the Tabuk Wing in trying to attack Al Asad airfield and the bridge over the Euphrates at As Samawah. On 27 February the weather cleared enough for LGB operations to continue. During the day the airfields at Al Asad, Shaykh Mazhar, Al Taqaddum and Habbaniyah were all attacked. In the evening, the last Tornado GR 1 mission of the war was flown from Tabuk against the airfield at Habbaniyah. It fell to Flt Lt M Warren and Flg Off Craghill to drop last bomb of the campaign, TIALD designated by Flt Lts W P Bohill and J W Ross.

In the early hours of 28 February came the news that Iraq had capitulated. 'We were all woken from our beds at 5 o'clock in the morning by the four-ship which had been cancelled due to Saddam's capitulation', recalled Flt Lt Marsh at Tabuk. It was the start of a party, which continued for the rest of the day. Marsh's feelings, probably shared with the other personnel, were 'about bloody time – it had started to drag a bit'.

Despite the surrender, the Tornado F 3 detachment continued to fly CAPs over Kuwait, albeit with a reduced number of aircraft available, as by now most of the fleet needed maintenance. The majority of crews took this opportunity to drop down to low-level to look at the destruction caused during the war. 'On a low-level sweep through the country, we were shocked at the devastation, particularly the complete destruction on the highway north', remarked Flt Lt Elliott. Strangely, the greatest threat now to aircraft flying over Kuwait was not SAM or AAA fire, but the thousands of vultures circling over the vast piles of wrecked vehicles and equipment on the road from Kuwait City north towards Basra. Flt Lt Ward was particularly struck by the precise bombing of the airfields in Kuwait; 'It was awesome. You could see an airfield, which formerly had HASs, destroyed. Every single HAS had a hole right through the top of it and all the maintenance facilities and hangars were just rubble.'

For Wg Cdr Moir 'the contrast between the precision attacks on the aircraft shelters at Ali Al Salem and Al Jaber airfields, and the devastation caused to the routed Iraqis on the Basra road was remarkable. The devastation in the oilfields was equally, if not more, dramatic, with

After the ceasefire, the Tornado F 3 crews were able to see first-hand the damage inflicted by Coalition fighter-bombers, such as these destroyed HASs at Ali Al Salem air base in Kuwait (*Paul Lightbody*)

TriStar tanker ZD951 of No 216 Sqn was based in Riyadh to support Tornado F 3 operations throughout the conflict, and it is seen here accompanying aircraft returning to Britain after the Gulf War (*Tony Paxton*)

burning oil wells stretching to the horizon and a canopy of dense smoke billowing over the desert.' The Tornado F 3 detachment continued its flying operations for a week, mounting the final CAP on 8 March. Four days later, 12 aircraft and crews returned to Britain, routing via a night-stop at Decimomannu, Sardinia.

Wg Cdr Moir commented that 'the return of the first Tornados to Leuchars was particularly remarkable because the weather had been perfect all the way back until we commenced our final descent to the airfield, where the cloud base was reported to be 200 ft and the visibility 1000 metres'. The rest of the aircraft and personnel returned home in the next few days.

The Tornado GR 1 detachments at Tabuk, Dhahran and Bahrain had stopped flying operations at the ceasefire. With the war over, RAF personnel at these bases were also repatriated as swiftly as possible. Sqn Ldrs Moule and Coulls led the first four Tornado GR 1s from Dhahran back to Brüggen, a flight which was, as Sqn Ldr Coulls related, 'an eight-and-a-half-hour trip with four AAR brackets. At the western end of the Mediterranean, we were given a sharp reminder of the fact that we were now back in a different regime when we met a tanker that had been flown out from the UK by a crew that had not been involved in the operation. During Operation *Granby*, we had, of necessity, re-written many of the routine peacetime procedures, not least for AAR. Therefore, we joined the tanker in a tactical formation and radio silent, and promptly – and quite rightly – received a severe ticking off from the tanker captain, insisting that we use the published procedures. Back to normality!'

However, six Tornado GR 1s remained at Bahrain to maintain a British presence in the region. These aircraft were flown by crews from Brüggen, many of whom had been part of the initial deployment the previous summer. Although, thankfully, there was no need for more operational flying, the crews at Bahrain were able to run a busy flying programme, with hi-lo-hi profile sorties into Saudi Arabia for 4-v-1 low-level simulated attack missions by day or four-ship parallel track auto-TF sorties by night. Most of these flights were supported by a Victor tanker, which was also based in Bahrain. The Tornado GR 1s remained here until May 1991.

A small detachment of Tornado GR 1s remained at Bahrain after the war. By then, the aircraft (including ZA463/Q ZD790/D, seen here) were showing signs of wear and tear, as well as staining from oil smoke in the atmosphere (*Tony Paxton*)

APPENDICES

TORNADO LOSSES

18 October 1990	ZA466 - Tabuk Wing
Caught raised barrier on approach, Tabuk	
Sqn Ldr I B Walker and Sqn Ldr R Anderson both ejected	
13 January 1991	ZD718 - Dhahran Wing
Flew into ground during OLF training, Oman	
Flt Lt K J Duffy and Flt Lt N T Dent both killed	
17 January 1991	ZD791 - Bahrain Wing
Shot down by SAM, Ar Rumaylah, Iraq	
Flt Lt J Peters and Flt Lt J Nichols both ejected PoW	
17 January 1991	ZA392 - Bahrain Wing
Hit ground during JP233 attack, Shaibah, Iraq	
Wg Cdr T N C Elsdon and Flt Lt R M Collier both killed	
19 January 1991	ZA396 - Bahrain Wing
Shot down by SAM, Tallil, Iraq	
Flt Lt D J Waddington and Flt Lt R J Steward both ejected PoW	
20 January 1991	ZD893 - Tabuk Wing
Crashed after control restriction, Tabuk	
Sqn Ldr P K Batson and Wg Cdr M C Heath both ejected	
22 January 1991	ZA467 - Tabuk Wing
Crashed during loft recovery, Ar Rutbah, Iraq	
Sqn Ldr G K S Lennox and Sqn Ldr K P Weeks both killed	
24 January 1991	ZA403 - Dhahran Wing
Damaged by own bombs, Ar Rumaylah, Iraq	
Flt Lt S J Burgess and Sqn Ldr R Ankerson both ejected PoW	
14 February 1991	ZD717 - Bahrain Wing
Shot down by SAM, Fallujah, Iraq	
Flt Lt R J S G Clark ejected PoW and Flt Lt S M Hicks killed	

COLOUR PLATES

Notes – Tornado F 3s retained their Air Defence Grey finish. During the initial deployment, the aircraft of Nos 5 and 29 Sqns carried their normal unit markings. The aircraft which deployed with No 11 (Composite) Sqn did not carry unit markings, except tail letters with initial letter 'D' indicating No 11 Sqn. In-theatre, some of these aircraft were decorated with 'Desert Eagles' insignia on their tails. When the final detachment was taken over by Nos 29 and 43 Sqns, each squadron repainted one aircraft in its own markings. Before deployment to the Gulf region, Tornado GR 1s were resprayed in an all-over Desert Pink finish over their normal grey/green disruptive camouflage. During the course of operations, the Desert Pink was subject to fading and weathering. Unofficial 'nose art' appeared at all three bases. Initially, it was limited to mission tally markers stencilled beneath the cockpit – at Tabuk the symbols reflected the weapons load, while Bahrain used simple bomb symbols and Dhahran applied palm trees. Gradually, the artwork became more extravagant, and at each base adopted its own particular style. Towards the end of the conflict the mission tally markers were standardised at each base and repainted more neatly.

1
Tornado F 3 ZE736/CK of No 5 Sqn, Dhahran
The Tornado F 3s of Nos 5 Sqn and 29 Sqn (both normally based at RAF Coningsby) were the first RAF combat aircraft to arrive in the Gulf theatre after deploying from Akrotiri. This aircraft is armed in its standard 'war fit' of four AIM-9LI Sidewinder AAMs on stub pylons and four Skyflash AAMs under the fuselage. It is carrying 2250-litre underwing tanks. The No 5 Sqn markings comprised a red roundel flash and red tail band incorporating a green maple leaf.

2
Tornado F 3 ZE982/DP of No 11 (C) Sqn, Dhahran
The Stage 1+ aircraft of No 11 (C) Sqn were equipped with AN/ALE-40 flare dispensers attached to the engine doors and a Phimat flare pod that was typically carried on the starboard outer stub pylon. The aircraft were finished in Air Defence Grey and did not carry squadron markings, although some were decorated with the 'Desert Eagles' insignia on the tail, as shown here. Since the 2250-litre tanks were needed by the Tornado GR 1 force, the Tornado F 3s inherited the 1500-litre tanks in their place. This aircraft was destroyed in a fatal accident in 2009.

3
Tornado F 3 ZE763/BA of the F 3 Detachment, Dhahran

Reflecting the Tornado F 3 operation as two distinct squadrons (as opposed to the previous unified 'Desert Eagles' unit), two of the aircraft at Dhahran were repainted in the colours of Nos 29 and 43 Sqns. ZE763 was chosen to wear No 29 Sqn markings, with the tail letters 'BA' as the mount of OC No 29 Sqn, Wg Cdr Roy Trotter. The aircraft is depicted in the typical operational fit of 1500-litre underwing tanks, four Skyflash AAMs under the fuselage and three AIM-9LI AAMs and a Phimat pod on the stub pylons. After the Gulf War, the aircraft served with both Nos 43 and 111 Sqns at Leuchars.

4
Tornado F 3 ZE966/GF of the F 3 Detachment, Dhahran

When the Tornado F 3 detachment commander Wg Cdr Andy Moir decided to return one aircraft to No 43 Sqn colours, he chose 'GF' – this is the traditional mount of the OC of No 43 Sqn because the tail letters are an abbreviation of the squadron motto, 'Gloria Finis'. The aircraft is also depicted in an operational fit of 2250-litre underwing tanks, four Skyflash AAMs under the fuselage and three AIM-9LI AAMs and a Phimat pod on the stub pylons. This particular aircraft is preserved at the Tornado Heritage Centre at Hawarden airfield, Wales.

5
Tornado F 3 ZE199/W of the F 3 Detachment, Dhahran

This aircraft is typical of most of the Tornado F 3s flown from Dhahran during the Gulf War, which wore no unit or other distinctive markings. The aircraft is depicted as it appeared in the last days of hostilities, when it carried out CAPs over Kuwait. By this stage the 2250-litre tanks had been returned to the F 3 force. The aircraft is illustrated as it was flown by Flt Lt Jerry Ward and Capt Joe Lortie USAF on the F 3 Detachment's last CAP on 8 March 1991, carrying a typical war load of four Skyflash AAMs under the fuselage and three AIM-9LI AAMs and a Phimat pod on the stub pylons.

6
Tornado GR 1 ZA470/FL of the Bahrain Wing

The first deployment of Tornado GR 1s to the Middle East was on 27 August 1990. Aircraft were supplied by the RAFG squadrons, although crews were drawn from Brüggen and Marham. This jet was provided by No 16 Sqn, normally based at Laarbruch. It is depicted here newly painted in the Desert Pink camouflage scheme and with the 'ferry fit' of four 1500-litre fuel tanks that was used during the flight to Muharraq airport via Akrotiri.

7
Tornado GR 1 ZD718/BH of the Dhahran Wing

This Tornado GR 1 was provided by No 14 Sqn, normally based at Brüggen. The aircraft is shown it a typical 'training fit' with an outboard Skyshadow ECM jamming pod (shown) on the port outer underwing pylon and a BOZ-107 chaff and flare dispenser on the starboard pylon, 1500-litre underwing tanks inboard and live JP233 canisters on the shoulder pylons. Unfortunately, ZD718 flew into the ground whilst making a hard turn at ultra low-level during a work-up sortie in Oman on 13 January 1991, killing Flt Lts Kieran Duffy and Norman Dent.

8
Tornado GR 1 ZD845/AF *Angel Face* of the Tabuk Wing

A small number of ALARM-capable aircraft were deployed to Tabuk to provide SEAD support for wing operations. This aircraft, supplied by No 9 Sqn based at Brüggen, is shown as it appeared in late January 1990, loaded with three ALARM missiles on the shoulder pylons. Self-protection armament included AIM-9L AAMs on the wing inner stub pylons. The artwork applied to the jet is modest by Tabuk Wing standards, with the name *Angel Face* painted on the starboard side only along with the names of the servicing teams. This aircraft was destroyed after the war when it experienced a rear fuselage fire during an air test on 26 February 1996.

9
Tornado GR 1 ZD748/AK *Anola Kay!* of the Tabuk Wing

Like many of the aircraft at Tabuk, this aircraft sports a shark's mouth. The artwork for this ALARM-capable aircraft, which had served with No 9 Sqn at Brüggen, was painted by Paul Bellis, one of the servicing crew at Tabuk. The aircraft is armed with 1000-lb freefall bombs, which were used for both low-level missions, during which the weapons were delivered from a loft profile, and later for medium-level operations until the introduction of LGBs into theatre.

10
Tornado GR 1 ZD739/AC *ARMOURED CHARMER* of the Tabuk Wing

This Tornado GR 1, which was originally from No 9 Sqn at Brüggen, was one of the TIALD-capable aircraft that provided laser designation for LGB attacks delivered by the Tabuk Wing. The TIALD pods were named 'Sandra' and 'Tracy' after the 'Fat Slags' characters in the comic *Viz*. Rather than the 'bomb' symbols recording such missions, TIALD sorties were marked with laser hazard symbols. The aircraft is shown configured with 1500-ltr underwing tanks in order to better show detail of the TIALD pod. More typically, it would have been configured with 2250-litre tanks for operational sorties.

11
Tornado GR 1 ZD744/BD *Buddha* of the Tabuk Wing

From 10 February 1990, most missions flown by the Tabuk Wing saw its jets tasked to drop LGBs. ZD744, which was originally from No 14 Sqn at Brüggen, is shown in a typical stores fit for these operations, with 2250-litre underwing tanks, AIM-9Ls on the stub pylons, ECM pods on the outer wing pylons and three LGBs on the shoulder pylons. Many of the Tabuk Wing aircraft were adorned with shark's mouth markings, and mission tally markers were initially painted in white. However, towards the end of the war, they were standardised and repainted in red.

12
Tornado GR 1 ZA447/EA *MiG Eater* of the Tabuk Wing

The aircraft (originally from No 15 Sqn at Laarbruch) is shown here late in the Gulf War carrying three Paveway LGBs, ECM pods, AIM-9Ls and 2250-litre underwing tanks. It had been christened *MiG Eater* after its first JP233 mission against Al Asad on 17 January 1990. During that night low-level sortie, Sqn Ldr Pete Batson and Wg Cdr Mike Heath caught an IrAF Mirage F1EQ (rather than a 'MiG') in their JP233 weapons footprint when it landed on the runway during their attack run.

13
Tornado GR 1 ZA465/FK *FOXY KILLER* of the Tabuk Wing
The aircraft is depicted as it appeared on 18 February 1991 during a six-ship attack against the Ar Ramadi highway bridge. It was flown by Flt Lt Mike Warren and Flg Off Mal Craghill and configured with 2250-litre underwing tanks, AIM-9Ls, ECM pods and three LGBs. The mission tally markers (which feature JP233, LGB and conventional bomb silhouettes) were later tidied up and repainted. The aircraft was originally on the strength of No 16 Sqn, based at Laarbruch, and after the Gulf War it served with Nos 17, 617 and 12 Sqns. ZA465 is now preserved at the Imperial War Museum, Duxford.

14
Tornado GR 1 ZD746/AB *ARSE BANDEET* of the Tabuk Wing
Shortly after being christened by its groundcrew, this aircraft, also from No 9 Sqn at Brüggen, was renamed *Alarm Belle*. Apart from being more politically acceptable, the new name reflected its capability as an ALARM-carrying aircraft. The jet is shown here in its operational fit, with 1500-litre underwing tanks, AIM-9Ls on the stub pylons and outboard ECM pods. During early ALARM missions, three missiles were carried, but on later sorties, as the number of operational Iraqi anti-aircraft systems decreased, this was reduced to two rounds.

15
Tornado GR 1 ZD792/CF *Nursie* of the Dhahran Wing
Unlike the aircraft of the Tabuk Wing, which sported colourful artwork and were named according to their tail letters, the Dhahran-based Tornado GR 1s were more modestly decorated. Some were simply named after characters in the television series *Blackadder*. This aircraft, originally from No 17 Sqn based at Brüggen, is shown loaded with 1000-lb freefall bombs. Freefall weapon loads varied from eight bombs, all carried on the shoulder pylons on Twin Store Carriers, to five bombs (only possible for those, mainly ex-Laarbruch, aircraft with a centreline pylon) or four bombs.

16
Tornado GR 1 ZA374/CNN *Miss Behavin'* of the Dhahran Wing
Reflecting both the prominence of the American new channel CNN during the Gulf War and the sense of humour of the groundcrew, an extra 'N' was added to ZA374's original aircraft tail letters 'CN' – another jet was repainted with the letters 'SKY'. The *Miss Behavin'* artwork that subsequently adorned the aircraft later in the campaign was painted by Flt Lt Paul 'Corky' Cawthorne and based on a photograph from a Pilots' Pals calendar. Depicted here carrying a bomb load of 1000-lb freefall bombs, ZA374 originally served with No 17 Sqn at Brüggen. It was later presented to the National Museum of the USAF at Dayton, Ohio, where it is displayed in its Gulf War colour scheme.

17
Tornado GR 1 ZA473/FM *Foxy Mama* of the Dhahran Wing
The artwork on this Tornado GR 1, originally from No 16 Sqn at Laarbruch, reflects its initial deployment to Tabuk. It was transferred to Dhahran as a replacement aircraft on 5 February 1991 and, while flying the jet ten days later, Flt Lts Kev Turnbull and Wally Grout dropped the 1000th RAF 1000-lb bomb of the conflict on storage tanks at Basra. It is loaded with 1000-lb freefall bombs, although these are fitted with Mk 117 retard tails (with the retard mechanism disabled) because all the Mk 114 tail units had been used. Although LGBs were used for an increasing proportion of bombing attacks

after their introduction into the theatre, freefall weapons were also employed on large area targets.

18
Tornado GR 1 ZD715/DB *LUSCIOUS LIZZIE!* of the Dhahran Wing
The name on this aircraft (originally from No 31 Sqn at Brüggen) was apparently inspired by Brüggen schoolteacher Liz Wren, who was also an honorary member of No 31 Sqn. The jet's artwork, however, is not indicative of her sense of dress. At Dhahran, operational missions were recorded by palm tree symbols painted under the cockpit, although a bomb symbol was used in some cases to record LGB drops. The aircraft is depicted here armed with LGBs and configured with 2250-litre underwing tanks, AIM-9Ls on the stub pylons and a Skyshadow ECM pod (shown) and a BOZ-107 chaff and flare dispenser on the outboard pylons.

19
Tornado GR 1 ZD740/DA *DHAHRAN ANNIE!!* of the Dhahran Wing
The artwork for this aircraft, from No 31 Sqn at Brüggen, was inspired by its tail letters – 'DA' was the aircraft traditionally allocated to the squadron CO. It is shown in the typical operational fit towards the end of hostilities, with 2250-litre underwing tanks, AIM-9Ls on stub pylons, ECM pods and a weapons load of LGBs on the under-fuselage shoulder pylons. The last operational mission by this aircraft was flown by Sqn Ldrs Douglas Moule and Chris Coulls against Habbaniyah airfield on 27 February 1991.

20
Tornado GR 1 ZD745/BM *BLACK MAGIC!* of the Dhahran Wing
This aircraft sported one of the more extravagant nose artworks at Dhahran. ZD745, which served originally with No 14 Sqn at Brüggen, completed 38 operational missions during the Gulf War. It is depicted at the end of the conflict loaded with 2250-litre underwing tanks, AIM-9Ls on stub pylons, ECM pods and a weapons load of LGBs on the under-fuselage shoulder pylons.

21
Tornado GR 1 ZD847/CH *Where Do You Want It?* of the Dhahran Wing
Featuring another piece of artwork by Flt Lt Paul Cawthorne (once again based on a Pilot's Pals calendar pin-up), this Tornado GR 1 originally served with No 17 Sqn at Brüggen. The aircraft is depicted as it would have appeared on 12 February 1991, on its second LGB mission, when it was flown by Flt Lts T Stout and C Mitchell during yet another attack on Al Asad airfield. ZD847 is configured with 2250-litre underwing tanks, AIM-9Ls on the stub pylons, and ECM pods and two LGBs on the shoulder pylons.

22
Tornado GR 1 ZA471/E *Emma* of the Bahrain Wing
Artwork for the Bahrain Wing aircraft was generally based on a large 'pin-up' image on the port side, with a name reflecting the aircraft tail letter. Thus, Tornado GR 1 'E', originally from No 15 Sqn based at Laarbruch, became *Emma*. The aircraft were also decorated on the starboard side with 'Snoopy Airways' cartoons featuring the Charles Schulz figure 'Snoopy' riding on a different weapon, in this case a 1000-lb freefall bomb. The aircraft is depicted relatively early in the conflict, loaded with 1000-lb bombs.

23
Tornado GR 1 ZD892/H *Helen* of the Bahrain Wing
This aircraft was formerly 'AF' of No 9 Sqn based at Brüggen. Apart from the 'Helen' pin-up, the aircraft also carried a 'Snoopy Airways' cartoon featuring 'Snoopy' on an AIM-9 AAM – again, this was on the starboard side only. It is depicted relatively early in the conflict, loaded with 1000-lb freefall bombs. By the end of the conflict there was an impressive tally of 31 missions recorded on the panel next to *Helen*.

24
Tornado GR 1 ZA475/P *Triffid Airways* of the Bahrain Wing
One of two aircraft at Bahrain painted with the *Triffid Airways* titling, this aircraft had previously served as 'FC' with No 16 Sqn at Laarbruch. It also had a shark's mouth painted on the starboard side. The aircraft is shown armed with BL755 cluster bombs under-fuselage. Although aircraft were loaded with these weapons on a number of occasions, they were not actually used operationally. After post-Gulf War service with No 12 Sqn, this Tornado was preserved as the 'Gate Guardian' at Lossiemouth.

25
Tornado GR 1 ZA491/N *Nikki* of the Bahrain Wing
Following the convention at Bahrain of naming aircraft according to their tail letter, this ex-No 20 Sqn (Laarbruch) Tornado GR 1 was christened 'Nora Batty' but the name was soon altered to *Nikki*. On the port side, the 'Snoopy Airways' cartoon depicted 'Snoopy' riding an LGB. By the end of the war, a second panel of mission tally markers was painted behind the pin-up figure. The aircraft is configured with 2250-litre underwing tanks, AIM-9Ls on the stub pylons, ECM pods and LGBs carried on the under-fuselage shoulder pylons.

26
Tornado GR 1 ZA399/G *Granny* of the Bahrain Wing
A number of Bahrain aircraft were painted with the titling *HELLO KUWAIT G'BYE IRAQ* before receiving further adornments. Aircraft 'G' (originally 'GA' of No 20 Sqn at Laarbruch) was also christened *Granny*. It is depicted in the typical operational fit for LGB operations, with 2250-litre underwing tanks and AIM-9Ls on the stub pylons, ECM pods and the weapons carried on the under-fuselage shoulder pylons.

27
Tornado GR 1A ZA371/C of the Reconnaissance Detachment, Dhahran Wing
Unlike the Tornado GR 1 bombers, the Tornado GR 1A reconnaissance aircraft were not, in general, painted with nose art other than the palm tree mission tally markers – this Tornado GR 1A completed 35 operational sorties. The aircraft is depicted in the operational configuration adopted for the first nights of the conflict, which included 2250-litre underwing tanks and two 1500-litre tanks carried on the under-fuselage shoulder pylons, giving a fuel load of about 11,000 kg – enough for long-range low-level reconnaissance missions to be flown without AAR support.

28
Tornado GR 1A ZA372/E *Sally T.* of the Reconnaissance Detachment, Dhahran Wing
The Tornado GR 1As were drawn from No 2 Sqn, normally based at Laarbruch. This aircraft was one of the few Tornado GR 1As to be decorated with a nickname (painted by Flt Lt Cawthorne), inspired by the wife of OC No 2 Sqn, Wg Cdr Al Threadgould. Unfortunately, it suffered from a number of unserviceabilities in the first week of hostilities and, as a result, it completed only 14 operational sorties. The aircraft is depicted with 2250-litre underwing tanks and AIM-9Ls on the stub pylons, as well as ECM pods.

29
Tornado GR 1 ZD790/D *Debbie* of the Bahrain Wing
A small number of Tornado GR 1s were retained at Muharraq after the Gulf War. Apart from the erosion of the Desert Pink finish, this aircraft, which had originally been supplied by No 15 Sqn at Laarbruch, was heavily stained by oil smoke in the atmosphere. On the starboard side it carries a 'Snoopy Airways' cartoon, with 'Snoopy' riding a JP233 canister. The aircraft is depicted in a typical training fit after the hostilities had ended, with 1500-litre underwing tanks, ECM pods, AAMs on the stub pylons and no under-fuselage stores. ZD790 had completed 39 operational missions during the conflict.

30
Tornado GR 1 ZD809/A *Awesome Annie* of the Bahrain Wing
Another of the aircraft carrying the *HELLO KUWAIT G'BYE IRAQ* titling, this Tornado GR 1 had originally served as 'BA' with No 14 Sqn at Brüggen. It flew 33 operational missions during the Gulf War. The jet is depicted as it appeared in Bahrain after the hostilities had ended – it was one of the Tornado GR 1s to remain in-theatre post-war. The aircraft later returned to No 14 Sqn, but was transferred to the Tornado Weapons Conversion Unit at Honington in the late 1990s. Unfortunately, it was destroyed in a crash on 14 October 1999 in which the crew was killed.

Spotless Tornado GR 1 ZD744/BD of the Dhahran Wing is loaded with two JP233s, while its port outer wing pylon carries a Skyshadow ECM jamming pod. This aircraft later moved to Tabuk (*Andy Glover*)

INDEX

Page numbers in **bold** refer to illustrations and their captions.